Six
RACY
MADAMS
of
COLORADO

Six RACY MADAMS *of* COLORADO

CAROLINE BANCROFT

BOWER
HOUSE

DENVER

Cover Design and Illustration by Margaret McCullough

Library of Congress Cataloging-inPublication Data on file.

A NOTE FROM THE PUBLISHER

The history of Colorado is the stuff of legend—full of bandits and fortune-seekers, treasure found and lost, racy madams and reclusive miners, all set in the beautiful and brutal Rocky Mountains. These stories are part of the American heritage; they are part of who we are and how we dream. They inspire the kind of books we publish at Bower House, like the titles by Caroline Bancroft in our Little Western Library series.

These books are old—in fact *The Unsinkable Mrs. Brown* was among the first biographies of "Molly" Brown ever written—but these books are worth reviving because the lore in them is truly timeless and they hit the bulls-eye of our mission. No one matches the wit and power of Caroline Bancroft; former president of the Colorado Folklore Society, she is the original, definitive voice of the Centennial State. An intriguing character herself, Bancroft writes her brief histories and biographies as if she were sitting on a log next to you, firelight sparkling in her eyes, a tin cup of hot cowboy coffee in her hand, spinning her tales with wit and authority.

Perfect for Colorado natives and newcomers alike, the Little Western Library series is a must-have for lovers of the mountains and of the people who made Colorado one of the most intriguing states in the nation. *Collect them all:*

The Unsinkable Mrs. Brown

Colorado's Lost Goldmines & Buried Treasure

Silver Queen: The Fabulous Story of Baby Doe Tabor

Six Racy Madams of Colorado

ACKNOWLEDGMENTS
Reprinted from the first edition

For Research Aid:
The Western History Department of the Denver Public Library have been invaluable aid, as always in my historical work. I wish to thank them collectively, but in particular Alys Freeze, Opal Harber and James Davis. Margaret Nowlen of the Bureau of Vital Statistics, Thomas Franck of the Probate Court, Lowell Hunt of the Supreme Court, Lorena Jones of *The Denver Post* and Colorado authors Forbes Parkhill and Ray Humphries all assisted generously. Others who helped were Royal Judd, John C. O'Flaherty, Archibald Morgan, George Harrison, Alexander Anderson, John Fisback, Robert Maiden, and numerous others in Denver who preferred not to be mentioned; W. T. Little and Marshall Sprague in Colorado Springs; Richard Johnson and Grace Sterrett in Cripple Creek; Steve Frazee in Salida; Louise Steel, Marie Skagsberg, Grace McDonald, Jack Lamar, Jack Mear, Harry Forman, Virgil Stauffer and Gilbert Gregg in Buena Vista; Maud Hall in Florence, and Arthur Mink and Marjorie Christie in Canon City. Jo and Fred Mazzulla took me to call on Lillian Powers and Laura Evans in 1952 long before I contemplated attempting this booklet.

For Photographs:
James Davis of the Western History Department deserves the greatest credit for locating possible pictures and for cheering me on. I am indebted to him for most of the illustrations. Louise Steel and Joanne Grieb of Buena Vista supplied three; Daniel K. Peterson, five; the Fred Mentzers of Cripple Creek, four; the Jo and Fred Mazzulla Collection, three, Nolie Mumey, one; the art department of the University of Denver, five; Don Bloch, one; and there were a couple of anonymous donations.

For Criticism:
Beatrice Jordan has applied for fine taste and astuteness in suggesting stylistic changes.

For Proofreading:
Shirley McFadden (Mrs. Bryant), a loyal and helpful friend, has taken time to catch errors of style or printing.

My gratitude goes to all, as well as apologies that this work is probably not as accurate as my usual productions. The shady ladies covered their tracks too well! A better booklet might have been written years ago before time had allowed grass to grow obscuring the paths they walked.

C. B.—1965.

The Author

The late Caroline Bancroft was a third generation Coloradan who began writing her first history for *The Denver Post* in 1928. Her long-standing interest in western history was inherited. Her pioneer grandfather, Dr. F.J. Bancroft, was a founder of the Colorado Historical Society and its first president.

His grandaughter carried on the family tradition. She is the author of the interesting series of Bancroft Booklets, *Silver Queen: The Fabulous Story of Baby Doe Tabor, Famous Aspen, Tabor's Matchless Mine and Lusty Leadville, Augusta Tabor: Her Side of the Scandal, The Unsinkable Mrs. Brown, Colorful Colorado, Unique Ghost Towns, Colorado's Lost Gold Mines and Buried Treasure,* and *Grand Lake: From Utes to Yachts.*

A Bachelor of Arts from Smith College, she later obtained a Master of Arts degree from the University of Denver, writing her thesis on Central City, Colorado.

She is shown here in a Metro-Goldwyn-Mayer photo, taken when the movie *The Unsinkable Molly Brown* was being filmed near Telluride, Colorado, in September 1963. The cameras and boom used on location may be seen in the background. The author is posed with Harve Presnell, the male lead who played Leadville Johnny, a fictionalized character bearing no relation to reality. Miss Bancroft's biography gives the true story of the unsinkable lady from Colorado and makes an amusing contrast with the legend.

Amusing Prologue

"You know, you look like an old friend of mine—Jennie Rogers."
The speaker was Phillip McCourt, one of the younger brothers of Baby Doe Tabor, and I was talking to him about his sister's life.

Phillip had been the building and box office manager for the Tabor Grand Opera House in the late 1880s and early 1890s during the period that his older brother, Peter, was the general manager. Phillip occupied a bachelor apartment upstairs in the opera house building at 16th and Curtis Streets. In those far-off Denver days he had the reputation of being quite a gambler and something of a gay dog when not on duty.

But that was all changed now in May, 1937. His dark hair and dashing moustache were gone. His hair was silvered and thin, and his frame, spare. He was seventy-eight years old (born November, 1858), and he lived as an old-age pensioner in a run-down room high in the old Windsor Hotel at 18th and Larimer Streets—the same formerly magnificent hotel where his brother-in-law, the Silver King, Senator Horace Tabor, had installed his bride, Baby Doe.

It was because I was writing a serial about Baby Doe that I was sitting there in the lobby of the Windsor, questioning her brother. The elderly beauty's body had been found frozen at the Matchless Mine in Leadville two years before, and I had been sent home to Colorado by an Eastern magazine to write her biography.

I had put off going to see Phillip until most of my field work and research were done because I had been told Baby Doe's brother would be taciturn and unhelpful. I found him reserved at first; but gradually he warmed up a little. Still I was surprised when he switched our topic of conversation to my looks.

"Oh, yes," I answered vaguely, "that's nice."
I did not know who Jennie Rogers was . . .

The passage of time altered my ignorance. Jennie Rogers was the most spectacular madam Denver ever had. Among a long list of notorious women operating parlor houses in the Mile High City's infamous red-light district which ran along Market Street (called Holladay Street before 1889), she was the only one who completely outshadowed the other Queen of the Tenderloin, Mattie Silks.

Both their stories are told in detail by Forbes Parkhill in his *The Wildest of the West*. Before the book was published, a number of local historians and writers were aware of Forbes' researches. I heard the name "Jennie Rogers" again and was told something of her story. Needless to say I was amused by my earlier naivete . . .

Phillip McCourt had died the year after our interview. I remembered that an old crony of his at the Windsor had been keeping a scrap book of miscellaneous items. Both men told me it included a clipping from *Godey's Lady's Book* which, they said, resembled Jennie Rogers.

2

It took me quite a little time and effort to run down what had happened to the crony and his scrapbook during the intervening dozen years. When I did, I was given permission to have two clippings copied (see pp. 8 and 36). You can see on page 8 why I was flattered to have had the old man think I looked like Jennie Rogers.

But when Forbes' book came out in 1951, my vanity was doused with cold water. The author printed a photo of the sculpture that adorned one of her parlor houses and wrote this caption:

"The full-bosomed stone Circe at the peak of the House of a Thousand Scandals is supposed to represent lovely Madam Jennie Rogers, leading figure in a story of blackmail and possible murder."

One day at a party I told Forbes my story, and ended with:

"Do I honestly look like Jennie Rogers?"

"Well, you don't have her real emerald earrings."

Very witty, I thought. Still I was left in doubt.

Sometime later, in November, 1952, I was taken to call on Laura Evans at her former parlor house in Salida. Again I asked.

"Hell, no," Laura answered emphatically. "You're better looking."

Then I told her about my interview with Phillip McCourt.

"Well, if Phil said so, it's true," Laura said. "Phil knew Jennie in her heyday. Later he was in love with the bookkeeper in Jennie's house. She was known as the Georgia Peach, and she was a friend of mine. But when I knew Jennie she was fat and not good-looking at all."

So there we are. We will none of us ever know the exact truth. According to Phil McCourt's crony, Jennie Rogers was the most beautiful madam of the 1880s. She was a tall, willowy brunette, nearly six feet tall, but "had a nice bosom." In those days her manner was vivacious and imperious, and she was a show-off when it came to horses or some exhibitionistic joke. Well, to be truthful, all these comments were applicable to me at the same age.

In 1950, Phil's crony commented again on our resemblance and directed me to other men who had known her, for by this time I was increasingly intrigued by our supposed likeness. As opportunity permitted, I looked up his friends and asked about Jennie. Through the years I have interviewed two score men who knew her, but not a single woman other than Laura Evans. This is a disappointment to me for I feel the real key to her character might be given through a feminine viewpoint. As it is, Jennie Rogers remains an enigma.

Amusingly enough, five more men volunteered the information, after the atmosphere was relaxed, that I reminded them of her or that I looked like her. These comments were offered in a shy embarrassed manner. I always smiled in answer, said I'd been told the same thing before, and that was how my interest in her and the subject of madams had been aroused. Then the ice was broken, and away we would go.

Or did we?

So many tales did not jibe, and the stories of Jennie and her rivals were so contradictory that I'm not sure. You must judge for yourself.

3

JENNIE
IN
STONE

The portrait of Jennie was carved by an unknown artisan in '88 when Jennie was aging.

CAROLINE
ON
CANVAS

The portrait of the author was painted in Paris by John Trubee when the sitter was 24.

Jennie Rogers, Denver's Immoral Queen

The red-light district of Denver in 1879 was already sensational. But it was to receive a new and larger sensation with the arrival of Jennie Rogers. Her legal name was Leeah J. Fries. (Note spelling— this was the way Jennie always spelled her own name. Some three dozen signatures which I have examined are consistent on this point. Incidentally, one writer has erroneously claimed that she could neither read nor write.) To say that the red-light district was sensational is to use rather Eastern and effete language. What any Westerner would have said at the time was:

"The Row is wide open."

Uniformly throughout Colorado the old-timers speak of "The Row" or "The Line" when they mean the street where the parlor houses, cribs, variety halls, saloons, gambling houses, and, in Denver, the opium dens congregated. In the earliest times this street tended to run parallel, a block away, to the main street. (Examples are Holladay, or Market, Street paralleling Larimer Street in Denver, Myers Avenue in Cripple Creek paralleling Bennett Avenue, and State Street in Leadville paralleling Chestnut.) But as the settlement grew, no matter whether it was a city, mining camp or cattle town, The Row tended to be left behind or to be forced to one side—against the mountain as in Aspen, or high on the hillside at the end of Pine Street as in Central City, or down close to the San Miguel River as in Telluride.

Although the parlor houses and cribs were generally mixed in the same block, there was a great distinction between the two. The cribs were single operations run by prostitutes in business for themselves. The crib lay-out in Colorado mountain towns was usually a frame building where a bedroom with a door and one window fronted on the street. A kitchen-living room was to the rear, and a privy stood out back, often on an alley.

In Denver, frequently the girls did not live in the cribs but at some nearby hotel such as the Bayonne, the Batione or even the Windsor. Some had husbands or steady lover-pimps with whom they lived in small frame houses not too far away from The Row. Consequently their reception rooms were on the streets, the bedroom next, and two or three cribs would share a mutual indoor lavatory at the rear.

The crib girls charged anywhere from 25c to $2, depending on their age and attractiveness. Usually the charge was $1 to which was added the profit on beer sold and perhaps a tip. If they prospered, they would move up in the world to the extent that they would buy a small house and have their names engraved on the glass transom of the door. (This practice was more prevalent in the mining camps than in Denver.) In the city the better crib girls built up a clientele that would follow them to a brick building with four or more apartments where each girl ran her own business.

Mostly, the crib girls preferred a street location where, dressed in low-cut short-skirted typical dance hall dresses, they would lean out the window to expose their upper charms or stand in the doorway to show the seductiveness of their limbs. In this way they could lure strangers into their cribs, give them satisfaction, and send them on their way. The girls' business was built on a quick-turnover principle.

The Denver parlor houses, on the other hand, operated on the principle of entertainment. The best houses would have two or three drawing rooms, each having a piano, in addition to a ballroom for dancing. A regular man piano-player was part of the establishment, and on busy nights extra musicians and entertainers were hired by the madam. The girls sat around the parlors on ottomans or stools, the comfortable chairs being reserved for the customers. They were dressed in ballgowns as rich and beautiful as one would see in high society, and their manners were often as good.

The charge for going up to a bedroom with a Denver parlor house girl was $5 for a "quick-date" or from $15 to $30 for spending the night, especially if there were any embellishments involved such as *soixante-neuf*. The madam's share of the take was half the set fee, permitting the girls to keep tips or to sell photos of themselves in their bedrooms. However, tipping seems to have been much less common in parlor houses than in cribs because the men felt they had already done adequate tipping downstairs.

During the joviality in the parlor or ballroom the charge for a bottle of beer was $1; for a split of champagne, $5; both plus tips, and the musicians were always tipped to play special numbers or just for the satisfaction of impressing the girls. In many houses the girls got a cut on the drinks and tips they promoted. By the time the customer went upstairs he was probably cleaned out.

The madam's share of the take was used to keep the house running, to hire the servants, to pay off the police, and maintain a liquor license (if the ordinance permitted the madam to have one).

Each day two good meals were served—what we would call "brunch" and an early dinner. In the best Denver houses the standard for meals was high. Filed among the papers relating to the settling of Jennie Rogers' will in the probate court of Denver is an $81 bill sent by her grocer, C. O. Green, for deliveries from October 1, 1909 through October 17 (the date of her death). Listed are steaks, chickens, rump roasts, eggs, cheeses, fresh fruits and vegetables, along with such delicacies as Worcestershire sauce and rum candies. The Windsor

Farm Dairy's bill for milk and cream during two and a half months was $42.50. No good madam such as Jennie stinted on her cuisine. The girls paid for board and room. The price varied from $5 or $6 a week in the early days to $15 or $20 in the last years of Denver's allowing The Row to operate. Their bedrooms were handsomely furnished in the style of the times. An important accessory was always the girl's own trunk. This constituted her safe, lock box and wardrobe for off-season clothes. Here were stored her cash and any personal mementoes she had chosen to treasure from that hidden past before she "turned out," as the saying was for becoming a prostitute. In the complete inventory of Jennie Rogers' 1950 Market Street house, all the bedrooms had enamel or brass beds, dressers, commodes, slop jars, rockers, straight chairs, rugs, lamps, lace curtains, and some even had writing desks. In the top houses the girls lived well.

From their share of earnings the "boarders" provided their own clothes. These were expected to be of the finest materials in the latest *haute couture*. Each girl had to have seven or eight evening dresses and two or three street or afternoon costumes which were frequently renewed. She was encouraged to use the madam's charge accounts for these purchases, and many of the madams received a kick-back from the modistes or stores patronized. The girls' clothes were often priced higher than for "good women" even without the extra markup designed for the madam. The girls seldom saved any money for the future.

Successful Denver madams, such as Jennie Rogers and Mattie Silks, made fortunes despite heavy expenses. Besides the normal bills for maintenance and repairs in owning and running a big house they employed a staff of Negro servants, a bouncer (who might be either white or colored), a regular piano player (who in the lesser houses sometimes doubled as the bouncer), and assorted additional musicians and entertainers. Furthermore, there were always the police who had to be payed off at all levels—sometimes on a "license" basis, sometimes on a "grease-the-palm."

The danger of being run into court for "operating a lewd house," as the charge generally put it, or being in trouble about liquor licenses was constant. (The ordinance varied through the years, sometimes allowing them a second class license but often revoking it.) Interference by the police with their liquor practices was a very serious matter because it was in this department that the madams made their real profit. Jennie's bill for wines, whiskeys and liquors from Sam Barets for three and a half months in 1909 was $310—a very sizable sum in those days, but for which she probably took in $3,000. The parlor houses of the nineteenth and early twentieth centuries were big business.

The women who succeeded as madams were a remarkable breed. They had to have ability for purchasing and management. They had to have tact and discretion in handling both police and customers. Every customer's name had to be preserved in strict secrecy even from

A PORTRAIT?

Copied from a scrap-book, this was one old-timer's idea of Jennie during her prime. After the change of life, Jennie put on weight and her pretty features coarsened. Until then, she remained extremely youthful in appearance with masses of dark hair. Late in life she dyed her hair which tended to harden her features. Her eyes were always big.

the girls. The unruly customers had to be persuaded to leave the house without a disturbance that might bring in the police.

In dealing with their "boarders" the madams had to have an expansive maternal instinct as well as the ability to discipline. Many of the girls were moody and frequently depressed enough to try the laudunum route to suicide—a real dampener to business. (Laudunum was a liquid opium that could be bought by the quart at any drugstore and was used as a pain-killer and tranquilizer by the tablespoonful. In large quantities it was lethal.) Many drank too much alcohol during an evening and became unattractive. These had to be let go as unprofitable. Others were temperamental and wanted to change houses repeatedly. (One method of preventing this was to keep the girl in debt to the madam for clothes.) Many more were fundamentally unstable. Yes, the madams had a host of problems.

Burdened with all these intricacies, they generally failed, if they did fail, on the score of their own personal loves. The madams, as

A LIKENESS?

This society photograph of the author was taken by Underwood and Underwood for a Washington newspaper when the author was thirty-four years old, two less than when Jennie first appeared in Denver. It would be improved if the subject had worn a girdle and brassiere instead of just panties and a dress. No hint thus of the well-corseted '80s!

well as the girls, were suckers for the type of men who could flatter, profess heartfelt love, and offer marriage (generally with an eye on the madam's fortune or the girl's earning capacity). Although the women had deliberately or inadvertently cast aside the world of respectability, most of the girls and some of the madams were gnawed by doubt and a longing for genuine love. They easily fell prey to the worst type of male, and Jennie Rogers was no exception.

But late in 1879, when the raven-haired Jennie first appeared in Denver, none of her doubts or longings were evident. She was a flashingly beautiful "wild one." A daredevil horsewoman who was full of life, Jennie faced Denver with defiant laughter. After she had looked the town over, she decided to stay.

When the Christmas holidays passed, she bought a two-story brick parlor house at 2009 Market Street from Mattie A. Silks, the then ruling queen of The Row. (Jennie's first Denver house still stands today. It is the buff-colored warehouse just south of the Cathay Post Bar and, except for a loading dock, retains its old lines.) The date of her purchase was January 15, 1880; the address in those days was 527 Holladay Street, and the price was $4,600 which Mrs. Leeah J. Fries paid in cash under her legal name.

Jennie's cash payment to Mattie Silks was part of the money she had made operating a house in St. Louis. In 1879 she was thirty-six years old and decided to sell out at a profit in order to move farther west. The mining camps were pouring forth fantastic stories of overnight wealth, and Leadville was at the height of its silver boom. The name H. A. W. Tabor was on everyone's lips. In the spring of 1878 he had been running a modest general store in the new camp and a year later, because of a lucky grubstake, was the richest man in Colorado. One of Jennie's customers told her the story in St. Louis, and she yearned to be closer to the source of such startling new-found riches.

In 1880 Denver had a population of 35,629 and was growing fast. Every day men struck it rich in the mining camps and moved down to town, many to build brownstone castles and cut a swathe. It was a time of prosperity and optimism at all levels of society and created just the right atmosphere for a rip-roaring red-light district. The Row was situated mostly from 19th to 21st on Holladay Street, now Market. There were also a few parlor houses and cribs scattered at other addresses easily accessible to Larimer, Denver's main street.

Before the year was out, Jennie's name began to make news. The following December, when her horse slipped on the frozen snow and rolled over on her on Holladay Street, the *Rocky Mountain News* described her as "well-known in this city." Dr. John C. Byrant ominously diagnosed her broken body to be "in precarious condition." He reckoned without Jennie's abounding vitality. By the following March she and a madam, called Eva Lewis, were being arrested for "unladylike conduct in the street" when their reckless horseback riding attracted too much attention. Strong and willful, Jenny was at it again.

Except for her predilection for showy horsemanship, Jennie's conduct was mostly dignified. She did not want the wrong kind of publicity. During the trial of a blackmailer, Peter Morahan, in May, 1882, it developed that, while a lesser Holladay Street madam was paying Morahan to get her name and picture in the national *Police Gazette*, Jennie had paid him $50 to keep hers out. Jennie was too good an operator to get involved with a man whom the *News* called a "reptile of the worst sort." A good madam wanted only word-of-mouth buildup by a fine clientele.

That is what Jennie had. Her business was far too brisk for her small quarters. She had already outstripped Mattie Silks in popularity and was cutting into the very rich exclusive business of Rosa Lee on Arapahoe Street. In 1884 Jennie built the largest and most substantial parlor house on Holladay Street, at an address that was to become 1950 Market Street in five years. Jennie had arrived.

10

Her house was a magnificent three stories high. On the first floor it had three parlors (one called the Turkish Room), a ballroom, dining room, and kitchen. Fifteen bedrooms were on the two upper floors. It was the first house on the block to extend solidly from the street to the alley. (Mattie Silks' two-story brick house at 1916 Market, toward the other end of the same block, ran only a little over half way the distance from street to alley.) In the basement of Jennie's new house was a primitive furnace (a real innovation), a wine cellar, storage closets, and servants' quarters.

Because of its substantiality and lavish furnishings, her executor finally sold this house for $5,500 more than her talked-of House of Mirrors, which she was to build four years later. Today 1950 Market Street is part of the AAA Furnace Company's offices, which have been constructed by combining her house and a parlor house she later leased at 1946 Market. Amusingly enough, the imprint of some of Jennie's original Victorian wallpaper is still visible on the north wall of what was 1950 Market. The pattern shows diamond-enclosed flowering tulips, and was undoubtedly gold on a color, most likely red or green—the color schemes described in the final inventory.

From that day in 1884 to 1909 she was the undisputed queen of the underworld. Other writers have placed the crown on Mattie Silks' curly head during a large portion of this quarter of a century. The unanimity of Jennie's obituaries in the four Denver newspapers and their appellations during the twenty-five years previous to her death would indicate differently. Also the testimony of men who knew them both confirms the fact that Jennie was the leading madam although not all the informants liked her as well as Mattie.

What sort of woman could grasp and hold the crown so long?

Everyone agreed that her business ability was excellent, and nearly everyone spoke of her manner which was described as "commanding," "having a good deal of authority" and the like. Most thought she had an attractive personality unless they were repelled by her weight and grossness in later years. Everyone was agreed that she never used foul language and that her English was better than many madams on The Row. Those who had known her earlier spoke of her good looks and everyone commented in one way or another on her being an "unusual person."

Jennie had been born in the country settlement of Allegheny, Pennsylvania, on the western outskirts of Pittsburgh, July 4, 1843. According to her death certificate, Jennie was the daughter of James Weaver, also born in Pennsylvania. (The informant was Leona De Camp, a fellow madam and great friend, who had formerly worked for Jennie in her famous House of Mirrors.) According to one obituary, her maiden name was Leah J. Tehme.

As a girl Leeah brought truck farm produce into town and worked in the markets of Pittsburgh where her early life was spent with the hucksters (as peddlers were called then). Even while a mere girl she

ADVERTISING

When Jennie Rogers was the most beautiful madam in St. Louis, she used to take her girls riding via four-in-hand coach. This, Jennie drove with expert horsemanship. Every eye was turned either on her or her horses or her pretty girls— all fine for business.

had many offers of marriage because of her beauty. She finally married a doctor whose name was probably Fries and settled down to a respectable existence. But the unselfishness and loneliness required of the wife of a family doctor who spent most of his days and nights making house calls and tending patients in his office were not to Leeah's liking. She wanted adventure.

Leeah ran away with a steamboat captain named Rogers. He had charge of a river boat running between Pittsburgh and Cincinnati and is supposed to have named his boat the "Jennie Rogers" after Leeah (the assumption being that the "J" in her legal name stood for Jennie). She probably never married him although they were accepted as man and wife for some years. At the time of her death the river boat "Jennie Rogers" was still in service on the same run.

Her next venture was as housekeeper at the mayor's house in Pittsburgh. This created a scandal, and political pressure was brought on him to get rid of her. He is said to have staked her to a new start in St. Louis where she opened what was euphemistically called in one of her obituaries "a fashionable resort." Her parlor house proved a great success, and here a man high in the police force, generally mentioned as the chief of police, fell in love with her—so much so, that after she moved to Denver, he made frequent trips west to see her.

Jennie probably had a home away from her parlor house soon after she began to succeed. Certainly by the 1890s many old-timers remember that she rented a shabbily painted frame house on the west side of Lawrence Street about three doors from the corner of 20th. Here, friends and relatives came to visit her. No doubt she received her St. Louis lover in some similar, if not identical, hideaway.

She may have used his name when she was arrested in 1884 "for vagrancy and for being a professional morphine taker." The *Rocky Mountain News* said her alias was Calvington, and that Judge George L. Sopris sentenced her to ten days in the county jail. Obviously Jennie was not a vagrant, and it is extremely doubtful that she was a professional morphine taker. Probably Jennie had been too hoity-toity to some member of the police force, and he had taken revenge. She may have bribed her way out of serving the sentence.

There is a story of this period, perhaps apocryphal, that the town council ordered all "the soiled doves," as they were frequently referred to in the newspapers, to wear a yellow ribbon indicating their occupation. Jennie Rogers, Mattie Silks, Lizzie Preston and the other notorious madams of The Row got together and ordered their girls to buy complete yellow outfits even to yellow parasols. Plumed and beribboned, they drove in buggies and hacks all around the downtown streets, flaunting the city fathers—who soon retreated in dismay and rescinded the order.

In the '80s Jennie was involved in a series of law suits and appearances in court. Unfortunately many of the details are lost. In August, 1881, she paid a $25 fine for keeping a "noisy and disorderly house." In May, 1882, she paid a fine and court costs of $224.05 for a friend, Mme. La Grange, who had had her seal skin sacque stolen, and then did not appear at the trial to give testimony against the thief. Mme. La Grange had "found times bad in Denver," gone to Gunnison where matters were equally bad, fell sick and in debt, and was unable to raise the railroad fare back to Denver for the trial. She was arrested on a writ of attachment, returned to Denver, fined, and saved by Jennie.

In 1886, an election year, when it was always an opportune time to stage a crusade against The Row, the newspapers were full of items. They ran from July through the December term of the Supreme Court. A July item was headed: "Raiding the Dens," and reported:

"The last few nights the police have been busily occupied among the houses of infamy, "pulling" those institutions, and the result has

13

been quite an increase in the sum paid over by the police court to the city treasury."

Not content with that, fifteen prominent "Keepers of Bagnios" were again raided in September and hauled into court "for keeping lewd houses." The *Denver Times* listed them all, including Jennie Rogers, Mattie Silks, Rosa Lee, Lizzie Preston and Minnie Clifford, among the best remembered. The newspaper added that the whole lot of "giddy girls of Holladay Street" pleaded "not guilty" and were forming a pool to test the matter of jurisdiction. (Denver was a part of Arapahoe County at that time.) Convicted in criminal court, they intended to carry the case to the Supreme Court. To head this movement, they chose Jennie Rogers as the most prominent and able.

The "giddy girls" were tried separately in criminal court, and most were convicted. At Jennie's trial her clever defense counsel trapped the district attorney into admitting that he had hired stool pigeons to get evidence. The *Times* added:

"Spectators at the trial were disgusted and said that the present means adopted to prosecute Holladay Street women was little short of blackmail."

Despite public indignation, Jennie was found guilty and fined $75 and costs.

Two days later a bit of drama occurred in court. Her attorney, aided by counsel for some of the other madams, had moved that sentence be suspended since the lawyers wanted to carry the case to the Supreme Court. All at once, Miss Jennie sailed in, her bustle bouncing with the vigor of her stride.

"I don't want to be the butt," she announced, her eyes flashing. The defendant insisted on paying her fine and court costs, plunking the money in gold and silver on the table from her reticule. Then the court dismissed her.

What happened after that is conjecture. Somehow she was overruled. Despite her refusal, the case of Jennie Rogers vs. The People was carried to the Supreme Court and there, as Number 1890 in the December term, was lost. Jennie had already paid her fine; the other "giddy girls" paid up, and Holladay Street continued as merry and boisterous as ever. No one objected because the election was over.

Two years later Jennie decided to expand further and wanted to lease 1946 Market to run in conjunction with her own house next door. At the time it was being leased and operated by her friend, Eva Lewis. The leased house did not lend itself very practically as an annex to 1950 Market because of the structure of the brick walls. A walkway between the two did exist at the rear, but Jennie decided it would make a better annex to 1942 Market, a frame parlor house, which was owned and operated by Minnie Clifford.

Miss Minnie had bought her house for $3,000 on December 23, 1880, eleven months after Miss Jennie opened her first house on The Row. By 1888 Minnie Clifford wanted to retire and in March leased

14

1942 Market to Jennie for $100 a month. Then in September Miss Minnie sold the house out from under Jennie for $10,000. That very same day Jennie bought the house from the new owner, Mary Leary, for $12,000, giving the first buyer a neat profit of $2,000 for a few hours' ownership.

In this year began the great unsolved mystery of Jennie's life. According to one story, her St. Louis lover knew of an early-day scandal involving a prominent Denver citizen. The police officer claimed this millionaire might have murdered his first young wife many years before in order to marry the rich woman who was married to his Colorado boss. The facts substantiated that the young wife did disappear, and the rich older woman did divorce her husband to marry his penniless employee. The second marriage had started the Denver citizen on the road to wealth and prominence. The lover was sure something terrifying could be effected with a skeleton planted in the millionaire's backyard and a fake warrant for murder.

Together, the police lover and Jennie hatched the details of this complicated melodramatic plot. They successfully blackmailed the citizen for $17,000 in order to build a pretentious brick and stone house, where Minnie Clifford's frame house had stood. Jennie hired William Quayle, well-known Denver architect, and a contractor to achieve her dream. The house would be so resplendent that Jennie would wrest the crown of Queen of the Red-light District from Mattie Silks and would then reign supreme.

THE POLICE GAZETTE GAVE ACCURATE REPORTS

This could very easily have been drawn at Jennie Rogers' house where the revelry was sure. Note the old boy who has caught a trim ankle.

SATURDAY NIGHT IN A DENVER, COL., BAGNIO.

There are several objections to this story. First, Jennie Rogers had long since acquired the crown. (The madams, themselves, had chosen her as head of their legal pool two years previous.) Second, the blackmail angle is vouched for by only one old-timer and is unknown to all others that were interviewed. Several remembered that Jennie's name was associated with this particular millionaire, but they thought of him more as a patron of her house and as an investment advisor when she visited him at his bank.

One informant had still a different story. He swore Jennie had borne this particular millionaire an illegitimate daughter who became a nun —all this having occurred before she came to Denver—and that was why he gave her the money for the house. I think this version most unlikely.

The reason these various tales may be important lies in the appearance of her house when finished. Five faces were carved in rose stone and used to decorate the greystone facade. Jennie was portrayed above the third floor window in the triangle formed by the peak of the roof—or at least a great majority of the old-timers insist that the face is hers. Above her face, sculptured with flowing locks, was a carved circular pediment. Today no one remembers what was on this disc. Four plain, somewhat phallic, pillars rose from the second floor roof line. At their base were four portraits in stone—two men, one young woman and what was probably an older woman, or possibly a fat boy.

Forbes Parkhill in his book believes these to be the story of the blackmail case. Stationed from left to right were the winking sensual face of the civic leader, his fat second wife, the murdered bride and the sorrowful divorced boss.

I am in total disagreement. The first two portraits bear no resemblance whatsoever in their grossness to the prominent couple, both of whom had refined, slender faces. In addition, the supposedly blackmailed man actually wore a Van Dyke beard, not mutton chop whiskers as in the sculpture. Far from being sorrowful, the supposed boss (in the pictures I have studied) is sticking out his tongue and ogling the young woman on the corner in what looks to me like greedy anticipation.

The old-timer, who insisted that Jennie had an illegitimate child by the millionaire, says that the young woman's face was her daughter's and that the cherub in the midst of a garlanded strip was really a baby's face—Jennie's baby. He says the other faces were from Jennie's faraway sentimental past and were known only to Jennie. He says none of the sculpture portrayed Denver people.

I am slightly more inclined to this opinion because several old-timers mentioned a daughter of Jennie's educated in the East. Not all thought the daughter was illegitimate, but rather the result of her first marriage. Conceivably Jennie might have wanted to immortalize her daughter and her Eastern past in stone.

16

JENNIE'S CONTROVERSIAL CARVED HEADS

The lovely madam, below an odd circle, presided above a winking man, a baby in a scrolled strip, a fat woman, a maiden, and an ogling man.

Still another interpretation of the sculpture was given by a man who took care of Jennie's high-spirited horses and her many vehicles. He said the faces were merely an advertisement of what was to be found within, the men's faces representing sly and sensual good times, the women's faces, bland secrecy and youthful allure. This explanation strikes me as very reasonable as does the explanation given by an old-timer interviewed in 1936 by Lee Casey (see p. 20) except this last man omitted one of the heads.

According to Forbes Parkhill, Jennie went back to the blackmailed banker and received an additional $780 because the estimate on the work had been too low. Despite her successful collecting of $17,780, she refused to pay the contractor his last payment and dared him to sue. Jennie is supposed to have boasted that no judge or jury would convict her and thus bluffed him out of his money.

The contractor must have been very gullible because there is on record only one legal case that she won. In the course of her expansion, probably early in 1888, she borrowed $6,350 from George T. Miles and gave a trust deed on two lots that she owned as security. These lots were across the street from her parlor house (running from 1959 through 1963 Market Street by later reckoning). Jennie paid part of

17

the debt, and then Miles made no effort to collect the remaining payments. Secretly he sold the lots. When Jennie discovered what had happened, she sued to recover her property and won the case in October, 1888. The court also relieved her of any further payments on the note because of the fraud attempted against her.

Two years previous she had instigated two suits; one for money against Jackson J. Lane, a stock grower, and another against Gracie Jerome, cause not given in the newspapers. Both cases were dismissed at her request without coming to trial, and she paid the costs. Undoubtedly both were settled out of court. In the case of Jackson Lane, he had probably engaged her house for a party and then not paid the bill. Jennie had a large following among cattlemen who came to Denver on business. It was their custom to entertain friends by making an exclusive arrangement with her to take over the whole lower floor for a particular night. On these occasions Jennie hired extra music and entertainment.

When Jennie's new house was opened early in 1889, it was the talk of the West. Soon it was given the nickname, House of Mirrors, because the parlor to the right of the reception hall was completely lined in mirrors. These were encased in golden bird's eye maple which was used throughout for the woodwork. Most of the furnishings of the room, including a grand piano, a marble-topped table and a love seat were also of bird's eye maple. The remaining pieces were of gilt and tapestry. Oriental rugs covered the parquetry floor and a crystal chandelier hung from a large circular mirror in the ceiling. The whole effect was of a sparkling lightness that glittered in a manner completely foreign to the usual heaviness and darkness of Victorian parlors, respectable or otherwise.

Plate glass doors at the rear led into the ballroom where more gold chairs lined the walls and another piano stood ready for merriment. Behind this ballroom were the dining room and kitchen. In the front hall a typical staircase of the times led to the second floor. It was of walnut with banisters. The walls on the way up and around to Jennie's suite on the second floor were lined with prints of horses. Her office-sitting room had a big window that looked out on Market Street. Here, sitting at an escritoire, she hired musicians for special parties, according to Alexander Anderson who played for her often.

Anderson and a friend had a mandolin-guitar duo with some accompanying vaudeville patter although mostly the boys were asked to play "hoe-down" music to dance to (such as "Turkey in the Straw"). Miss Jennie usually gave them $2 each for the night's work and a free dinner in the kitchen. Added to this were tips that the girls solicited from the men in the course of the evening. The boys could make more money by performing at Ryan's Saloon at 19th and Market or the Alcatraz on 20th, and passing the hat. But these places were so tough that they frequently had the whole take stolen from them. The boys learned to prefer the parlor houses.

JENNIE ROGERS CHOSE THE FINEST DRESSES

The modistes made handsome sales at the parlor houses and were glad to bring exhibits, often giving the madam a percentage in return.

When the House of Mirrors was opened, a formal entry way was built, connecting the house with 1946 Market. Jennie took over the lease from Eva Lewis (who moved to 1923 Market, a house opposite Mattie Silks) and Jennie operated the two houses as one unit. Likely she operated all three adjoining houses because it was not until two years later that she leased 1950 Market to Minnie Hall.

Jennie was at the height of her popularity and patronized by many big names. During the 1880s and early '90s the legislature was meeting at successive addresses on Larimer or Market Streets, never more than a block or two away from her house. David Mechling who ran a drugstore from 1887 to 1935 at 2001 Larimer, a block from Jennie's, recalled in the *Rocky Mountain News*:

"Each afternoon about three o'clock the august lawmakers would retire to Jennie Rogers' Palace of Joy on Market Street and there disport themselves in riotous fashion . . .

"Nothing was thought of that sort of thing in those days. It was a day of hard living. Men took their liquor neat and women took what they could get their hands on."

Another old-timer was interviewed in 1936 by Lee Taylor Casey, influential columnist of the *News*. This man was commenting on the fact that many Market Street girls purposely chose their way of life:

19

"Like "Queen" Jennie Rogers whose mirror-parlor was the talk of the West and whose stone palace is still standing—a Buddhist temple today—with three beautifully sculptured heads set in the wall. Youth with its wide-eyed smile of innocence; Experience with tired eyes and no innocence; Disillusionment with features of ugly sneering cynicsm . . .

"No brazen hussies for the madams of The Row! They valued the never-failing allure of half-concealed charms . . .

"If the walls of "Queen" Jennie's house could speak! Some sinister tales, yes, with now and then a suicide, but mainly joyous. I believe I could catch in what was Jennie's kitchen a faint echo of big tin dishpans being beaten by young and lusty hands as we staged a night-shirt parade. The ladies were in high-heeled slippers, and not much else, singing with us *The Battle Hymn of the Republic.* To strident beats on the tin drums, we marched in the middle of Market Street, with everyone uproariously applauding and on to Mosconi's. There we had fat sputtering hot squabs on toast and pre-dawn coffee that steamed with Olympian nectar—now gone like all the rest—gone with youth and the "Ladies of Laughter."

Jennie was not always a "lady of laughter." Tempestuous and emotional, she had her melancholy days. It was then that she turned away from people to her great love for horses. As she grew older, she rode less and drove more—particularly a span of matched high-stepping bays, hitched tandem style. Driving them reminded Jennie of the fun she used to have handling her "advertising" coach in St. Louis, swinging the lead team in a wide arc and checking the wheelers. She still liked the feel of four reins in her hands.

Her love of horses led to the most long-time love of her life for a man, John A. Wood. In 1881 Jack was a twenty-three-year-old hack-driver who watched her antics with horses disapprovingly. He was a big gruff man, but his hands were gentle and his horses well-cared for. Jennie usually hired a hack when she went shopping or to a matinee at the Tabor Grand Opera House. Soon she formed the habit of patronizing Jack exclusively. He was unprepossing and very poor, owning no more than his hack and two elderly horses which he alternated using in order to save their strength. Yet there was something about him that she liked.

Sometime in the 1880s she suggested to him that he was foolish to spend his life in the open, braving the cold of winter and the heat of summer, and that, as a hack driver, he would never make more than a pittance. She offered to set him up in a saloon. Her interest in his welfare led to love, and soon to Jack's accepting her offer. Why they chose Salt Lake City as the site for the saloon is not clear unless Jennie was still involved with her police officer and didn't want the two to meet during the St. Louis man's visits to Denver.

After the saloon was opened, it proved a success, and Jennie made a surprise trip to Salt Lake to congratulate Jack. The trip proved a

SCULPTURE

Two of the heads that were on Jennie's parlor house have been turned into a decorative garden piece by Don Bloch. The man was the face at the far left corner.

surprise for both of them. Jennie found him in the arms of another woman. She whipped out a pistol (which madams of the period usually carried as part of their business) and shot him. Jack was wounded, and Jennie was immediately apprehended by the police.

"Why did you do it?" they demanded.

"Because I love him," was Jennie's classic reply.

Love or not, that was the end of the romance. Jennie returned to Denver and applied herself to business affairs, which may or may not have included blackmail.

Her business deals did include buying a whole half block of lots in Sloan's Lake Heights as an investment. During the '80s there was a trend for fashionable people to build mansions in what was called North Denver, or the Highlands, and it appeared that Denver was going to grow in that direction. She also bought shares in an irrigation and reservoir project in Logan County near Sterling. This move was suggested by one of her cattlemen customers who foresaw the decline of cattle spreads and the growth of agriculture along the South Platte. Both investments promised to be profitable. Her decisions showed much more astuteness than the habit of most madams who put their profits into parlor house and crib real estate.

The House of Mirrors was only one of her imaginative projects; yet all were unsatisfying. After the excitement of its completion had worn off and after even such big names as Marshall Field of Chicago had paid her visits to congratulate her, she was unhappy. She was forty-five years old and she was still in love with Jack Wood.

It was some two years since her Salt Lake trip. Jennie knew from the underground that Jack had recovered, sold out in Salt Lake and moved to Omaha where he was operating a saloon with a partner. A young man who was intrigued with one of Jennie's girls happened to be in Omaha on business and met Jack Wood's partner. The partner revealed to the young man that Jack was still in love with Jennie and regretted deeply the whole Salt Lake scandal.

When the young man returned, he called at the House of Mirrors, and Jennie made a point of questioning him about Omaha. The young man made a bet with her that if she would write to Jack, he would answer. Jennie was sure he would not. Jack had always been critical of her slashing out in a temper at her horses. He would be even more unforgiving of the rage that made her shoot him.

But Jennie was a natural gambler—she always bought the Chinese lottery tickets sold in Hop Alley—so she took the bet: a sealskin cap against a plumed hat. She wrote the letter. Jack answered, and she lost the bet.

A fairly regular correspondence developed between the two, and by July 4, Jennie's birthday, Jack was suggesting that he take his August vacation in Denver. Jennie was delighted and received him at her hideaway. Jack proposed marriage; the young man who won the sealskin cap agreed to stand up with the bridegroom, and Jack and Jennie were married August 13, 1889. When Jack's vacation was over, he went back to Omaha to business, and Jennie continued with hers, both amassing wealth in their individual occupations.

The marriage, though unconventional, was a happy one. His visits to her Lawrence Street hideaway are remembered as being fairly regular, and her absences from Denver were frequent. Presumably she was in Omaha or taking trips with him. In February, 1896, Jack Wood died at the age of thirty-eight. We know none of the details because the state of Nebraska did not start the practice of death certificates until 1904. Neither do we know if Jennie was there, but we do know she had his body returned to Denver and interred at Fairmount Cemetery. She chose an eight-foot high monument, supported by four Corinthian columns, bearing the legend, "He is not dead but sleepeth" and a large deep carving *J. A. Wood.*

In the eight years of their marriage it was definitely "business as usual," and Jennie may have inherited a substantial estate from Jack. Not that she needed it, because her own business continued at full speed (after a slump during the Silver Panic years of '93 and '94).

22

In 1891 she lessened her responsibilities by renting 1950 Market Street to Minnie A. Hall, who may have taken Jennie's lease on "1946," too. Certainly some such arrangement is indicated by the 1892 advertisement in the *Denver Red Book: A Reliable Directory of the Pleasure Resorts of Denver.* This little pocket-size pamphlet was issued for the benefit of the Knights Templar convention in August. The convention was the biggest Denver had yet had and was timed to correspond with the opening of the Brown Palace Hotel. The Row was expecting plenty of patronage.

Miss Minnie advertised "30 Rooms, Music and Dance Hall, Five Parlors and Mikado Parlor, Finest Wines, Liquors and Cigars, 20 Boarders and a Cordial Welcome to Strangers." Since we know that 1950 Market had only fifteen bedrooms, two parlors, a Turkish Room and a ballroom, either Miss Minnie was exaggerating or she had an annex house under lease (although not necessarily next door).

Jennie's House of Mirrors was represented by the simple statement: "Ella Wellington, 1942 Market, Everything First-Class." Jennie undoubtedly did not want to use her own name and so used that of her bookkeeper. Ella Wellington may easily have been "The Georgia Peach," sweetheart of Phillip McCourt and friend of Laura Evans, because this was close to the time Laura was working in Denver. Mattie Silks apparently had not taken an advertisement, either under her own name or her bookkeeper's, probably because Mattie's house was so arranged that her regular clientele was all she could handle.

In 1894 the city directory listed Miss Jennie Rogers' residence as 2005 Market, the corner house next door to her first little house. Why, I don't know. She may have bought or leased this house as a further part of her expansion. Jennie was always "wheeling and dealing"— borrowing large sums of money (some of these sums at exceedingly high rates of interest) to achieve a new ambition, and then selling off property to attempt something else. The next two years she is listed back at the House of Mirrors and business as usual.

Outcries for political reasons against The Row continued during the '90s as in the '80s. In October, 1895, the *News* was boiling with indignation because the gang ward heelers were causing an "undeniable degradation of womanhood." The gang committeeman of lower Denver vouched for what he said were forty nice respectable voters. The *News* printed all forty names with heavy sarcasm. The list included Mattie Silks, 1916 Market, and Leah Wood, 1942 Market. To the ire of the *News*, this man was forcing "the fallen" to appear at the polls with pure wives and daughters.

In the 1897 city directory Miss Jennie Rogers, as such, is gone. Since the directories often refer back a year in fact, and since 1896 was the year that Jack died, she must have given up business to nurse her grief. The House of Mirrors was definitely leased to Lizzie Preston, an older established madam and long-time friend. Lizzie Preston had operated a house at 1715 Market Street for nine years and then for

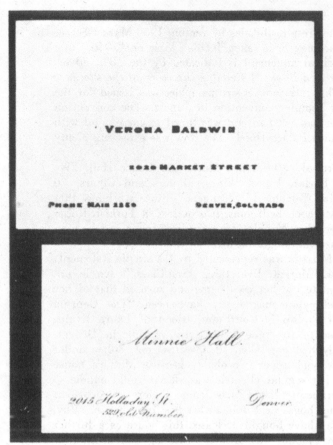

TOP MADAMS

These were the discreet cards that the madams used for promotion. Verona's is later than Minnie's. Minnie leased "1950" from Jennie for fourteen lucrative years.

five years in the mid '90s was involved in a "hog ranch" out of town. Jennie knew Lizzie could make a success of the House of Mirrors and its annex. Both Mrs. Jennie Rogers and Mrs. J. A. Wood were listed as rooming at 1921 Lawrence Street (which is one lady at a hideaway, no doubt, resting and guarding her deteriorating health). In the 1898 directory, she is gone completely — probably visiting her relatives in the East.

Then Jennie is back again. In 1899 her listing is for 2016 Market, followed by three years at 2020 Market. These addresses were actually for the same parlor house, a big two-story affair with two entrances, pictured in Forbes Parkhill's book. Across the street at 2015 Market (The Cathay Post Bar now) Verona Baldwin, the San Francisco beauty who had shot her cousin, "Lucky" Baldwin, was operating a house selected on her arrival in Denver in 1898. After Jennie gave up 2020 Market, Verona changed over and operated "2020" for nine years. Whether Jennie owned or leased "2020," is unknown, but I do know her own two houses, "1950" and "1942" were under lease during these four years to Minnie Hall and Lizzie Preston.

24

Apparently she was happy in Denver at this period because in May, 1899, she gave an interview to the News in which she said she was investing in property above Welton Street along 16th and 19th Streets. She explained that she believed in the future of Denver. Her eventual purchase was a building across from the then St. John's Cathedral, at 20th and Welton Streets, which had store space on the first floor and rooms on the second—good rental property.

But by 1902 she had other fish to fry despite the fact that Market Street was booming. The Denver Republican for March 17 said: "There is no longer any Sunday on Market Street. "The Row" yesterday afternoon was busier than ever. More than half the cribs were occupied by half-clad, painted women, shouting invitations to the passersby, some of them with the casements open, leaning out into the street. Every barroom was open and women were carrying pails of beer to and fro. Crowds of half drunken men and women were laughing and drinking together inside every building, even the shaded bagnios. All were brazenly ignoring the policemen who walked up and down, oblivious to the glaring violation of the laws."

Nonetheless, Jennie decided to leave for Chicago. Always emotional, her decision may have been influenced by two factors other than ambition. She had been devoted to a pug dog, which she had owned for more than ten years, and the dog died. In excessive sorrow Jennie had him buried in a gold casket. Also, Dr. Hugh Taylor had warned her that the attacks she had been having of violent headaches and nausea were from chronic Bright's disease. Jennie had been subject to these attacks for some years. But each time she would recover completely and refuse to take the doctor's advice for long. He warned her that her kidneys were seriously affected.

Despite her defiant attitude Jennie knew the doctor must be right because her weight problem, her breathlessness, the swelling of her ankles, the puffiness under her eyes, and difficulty in seeing were all on the increase. Jennie may have decided that a lower altitude would put less strain on her heart and high blood pressure. Dr. Taylor had told her she should not drink. It was almost impossible to cut out alcohol in her business, but imbibing seemed to affect her less when she went to see her niece in Cincinnati or her sister in Pittsburgh—both cities with low altitude.

In October, 1902, Jennie borrowed $15,000 from a Juliette Fammeree (sounds like a madam's name) and bought a lavish parlor house in Chicago and a palatial home in an exclusive residential district of Cook County, Illinois. She put up the property as security. By the time of her death, Jennie's note to Juliette Fammeree had been reduced from $15,000 to $6,000. The property Jennie bought was worth between $35,000 and $40,000. To get the cash for the down payments she sold her store building in Denver and her emerald earrings.

For years these emerald earrings had been Jennie's trademark. She never revealed if she had bought them for herself or if they had been

NEW BEAU

Jennie's Chicago parlor house was soon being visited regularly by Archie Fitzgerald who displayed more interest in the madam than in the attractive girls. He knew that she was a wealthy woman.

a gift. Old-timers remember seeing her wear them as long as she retained her looks. With the increasing edema from her Bright's disease, she put them aside, and finally sold them.

Now began another strange chapter in Jennie's life. At her parlor house in Chicago she met a thirty-seven-year-old contractor, Archibald T. Fitzgerald. He was more than twenty years younger than she. *The Denver Post* printed a profile photograph of him in which he seemed a coarse type with a heavy black moustache, dark eyes, a double chin and a definitely receding dark hair line. He started to pay court to Chicago's newest impressive madam—Jennie.

We know very little about Fitzgerald except that he gave her a diamond and ruby engagement ring and encouraged her to buy expensive carriages—a landau, a brougham and a victoria. He soon called frequently at her residence, and he and the coachman would deliver her downtown in these carriages for business at her parlor house. The couple also went for drives in the afternoon. He also thought "taking the waters" at Hot Springs, Arkansas, might be good for her health. They made several trips there, and on April 26, 1904, they were married in Hot Springs.

In April, 1904, (right after her marriage) Jennie was called back to Denver because of Lizzie Preston's death. She took rooms at 908 18th Street until she could find a new madam for the House of Mirrors. Again the madams played "musical chairs" as they seemed to do throughout the years. Etta Kelly, who had first been a girl under Jennie Rogers at "2020" and then for five years under Minnie Hall at Jennie's "1950," moved up to being a madam. Etta took over "1950." Minnie Hall who had leased "1950" for fourteen years from Jennie, went back to "2015" which she had operated once before during the year of 1890, before Verona Baldwin came to town. Etta Kelly, Jennie's new lessee, was a very "societyish" madam and ran an enterprising house. Jennie stayed some months, seeing to repairs on her houses, and tending to business matters, and aiding Etta in her new role.

Not long after her return to Chicago Jennie was informed that Fitzgerald was already married. Fitzgerald insisted his marital affairs were clear, and that he had been divorced in Hot Springs on March 12, six weeks before he and Jennie were married. The Fitzgeralds continued to live together as a respectable married couple in Jennie's palatial home. Yet Jennie was increasingly doubtful of her legal status and unhappy with her choice.

By 1907 she was convinced that Fitzgerald was too sharp an operator even for her. She returned to Denver and took back the management of her houses. She chose the House of Mirrors to live in, and here she summoned Harry E. Burlew, private detective, to shadow Archie Fitzgerald in Kansas City. Jennie was convinced Archie was living there with one of his wives and that he was truly a bigamist. She signed business and legal papers, Leeah J. Wood, doubting that her name was Fitzgerald. If the Fitzgerald marriage proved to be legal, she was considering a divorce, but wavering.

Miss Jennie relinquished her lease on "1946" to Etta Kelly the following year, and next leased Etta the House of Mirrors. Jennie went back to Chicago for the latter part of 1908 and again joined Fitzgerald for a trip to Hot Springs. She was tired and cornered—truly "property poor." It was increasingly difficult to find good renters for either her residential property or her parlor houses. Without cash coming in, Jennie began to let bills slide. She longed for someone to care for her as Jack Wood had—not bleed her as Archie did.

Upon her return to Denver early in 1909, she borrowed several thousand dollars, part of which she put into renovating, re-wiring and refurbishing 1950 Market Street. She chose this house as her personal residence, which it had been before, from 1884 to 1889, when she was in her early forties and climbing fast. Now she was sixty-five and desperately fighting to keep up her courage. What happened to the rest of these large loans is unknown. Likely they went to her sister, Annie Smith, who was in indigent circumstances, or perhaps to Fitzgerald.

The money did not go for clothes or personal extravagances. During this year of 1909 she only bought one dress at Daniels and Fisher's for $35 and one suit at the Denver Dry Goods. Most of her expenditures were for the houses, such as having the draperies and lace curtains cleaned, carpentry repairs, including "a new mirror for Miss Jennie's dresser," and the $75 a month rent to Jacob Lang for 1946 Market (for which she was in arrears after June 1). Business was not as brisk as usual.

THE ASTOUNDING PARLOR OF MIRRORS

Collector Nolie Mumey saved the circular ceiling mirror, the chandelier and the small square mirrors, one of which hangs in my kitchen.

Jennie found herself increasingly hard pressed for cash, and borrowed a series of small sums from her friend, Leona de Camp. This pretty young madam operated 1952 Market Street, next door to Jennie on the north, having begun her Denver career in 1907 as a girl in Jennie's House of Mirrors. The women had become fast friends. Leona gave Jennie $25, $30, even $100 as temporary loans to meet interest payments, bribe the police, or stall off pressing creditors. Jennie was optimistic that with a little more time everything could be put to rights and Leona paid back.

In October this optimism collasped. Jennie had another attack, more violent than ever. She stayed in bed several days trying to still her pounding heart. Finally on Sunday night, October 10, when Leona came in to see how she was, they agreed Dr. Taylor must be called. He arrived about eleven o'clock and was gravely concerned.

"Am I in immediate danger?" Jennie asked.

Dr. Taylor hesitated briefly, then replied:

"Well, with your chronic Bright's disease, uremic poisoning could set in at any time."

Jennie did not hesitate.

"In that case, I have business matters to attend to. Would you please phone my lawyer?"

Attorney Stanley C. Warner arrived at 1950 Market about one in the morning and went up alone to Jennie's room while Dr. Taylor and Leona waited in the front parlor. After conferring with Jennie, Warner came downstairs and wrote out a will in a distinguished longhand. The will bequeathed everything to Jennie's sister, Annie Smith; a niece, Annie Smith Prestele, and a nephew, Albert Marsh Mariner. Warner named himself as executor. No mention was made of Fitzgerald in Chicago nor of another niece, Margaret J. Kinney, living in Pittsburgh.

When Warner had finished, all three went back upstairs to Jennie's room. Warner read the last will and testament aloud to Jennie, her doctor and her friend.

"That's just what I want," Miss Jennie said firmly. "Now please give me my glasses."

She sat up in bed, placed her glasses on her nose, dipped a pen in an ink well on her bedstand and signed, "Leeah J. Wood."

"Will you be good enough to witness it?" she asked, looking at the doctor and her friend.

Dr. Taylor signed with no hesitancy. When it was Leona's turn, she turned to Warner and asked how she should sign.

"With your legal name," he answered.

Leona wrote out clearly and plainly, "Margaret Rohan."

Dr. Taylor argued with Jennie, seconded by Warner and Leona, that she should be moved to a hospital. She finally agreed and the next morning was admitted to Mercy Hospital. She grew worse each day. For the first four days Miss Jennie wrote almost constantly, personal letters (which a nurse mailed to Eastern addresses), and business memos for Stanley Warner. After that her mind grew cloudy, and Dr. J. N. Hall was called in consultation. There was nothing to be done—uremic poisoning had set in. On Sunday, October 17, 1909, "Queen" Jennie Rogers breathed her last.

Our story properly ends here. But Archie Fitzgerald sued for one-half her estate. During the next twenty-two months Jennie's Denver attorney and her Chicago lawyer, Alfred E. Barr, battled for the validity of Jennie's will. The unsavory court contests, sensational newspaper accounts and strange twists of fate were as melodramatic and contradictory as if Jennie Rogers were still alive.

Finally Barr was instrumental in getting Fitzgerald to settle out of court for $5,000, the return of his diamond and ruby engagement ring, the letters he had written Jennie, and possession of all her handsome vehicles stored in Chicago. During this intervening period Warner had been leasing the House of Mirrors and "1950" and subleasing "1946" to Etta Kelly. The rent for all three was $500 a month. With Fitzgerald's capitulation he was finally free to settle the estate.

Warner sold 1950 Market with its furnishings to Etta Kelly for $19,500 and the House of Mirrors to Mattie Silks for $14,000. These were modest prices because harassment of The Row was now beginning to be serious and property values were declining. Jennie's irrigation bonds and Logan County land, supposed to be worth $50,000 were sacrificed for $2500. Her Sloan's Lake lots suffered the same fate. In all, her estate which had been valued at more than $200,000 some years before, proved to be worth around $82,000 with thirty-six claims against it that were settled for $20,500. This sum did not include Fitzgerald's $5,000, the lawyers' and executors' fees, their traveling expenses back and forth from Denver to Chicago, two state inheritance taxes, and sundry court costs. When all the shouting and tumult were ended, there was less than $30,000 for the three heirs to divide.

While the strife that Miss Jennie had started was continuing on, she was peacefully at rest beside her great love. Her sister and niece had arrived in time for the funeral. It was on October 22, 1909, and was conducted by one of the finest of the early Episcopalian ministers —Rev. Charles Marshall. The funeral was attended by nearly every madam of The Row, many of the girls, assorted tenderloin characters, her devoted Negro maid, and a smattering of respectable business associates. It must have been an entertaining and ironic sight to see this motley crowd gathered around Lot 76 in Block 2 at Fairmount. The plot is not more than three hundred feet from the chapel, in the center of the oldest and most dignified part of the cemetery.

The four-columned J. A. Wood monument is surrounded by those of many distinguished pioneer families. It faces south directly on the dirt driveway, separating Block 2 from Block 3, and must have had a nice view of Pikes Peak before the spruce trees grew so tall. Jack's

A NEW CUSTOMER COULD SAMPLE THE WARES

*Before choosing a bedroom partner, the gentleman might try a kiss
from each of a bevy of girls gathered in one of the ornate parlors.*

headstone reads, "John A. Wood; Sept. 27, 1857; Feb. 28, 1896,"
while Jennie's says merely "Leah J. Wood, Died, October 17, 1909,"
(thus hiding the fact that she was fourteen years older than he).

The three stones are artistic and extremely well-carved, as I am
sure the mistress of the House of Mirrors saw to very carefully—that
same enigmatic lady who embellished her parlor house with carved
stone sculpture.

What amuses me greatly is that the Queen of the Red-Light District
should be there in such stately and anomymous splendor, unsuspected
by passersby. Amusing me even more is the fact that the J. A. Wood
monument has an excellent view across the lane to the Bancroft monument in Block 3 and that Miss Jennie's headstone is but a stone's throw
away from a headstone that will read "C. B."

THE HOUSE OF MIRRORS BECAME A CHURCH

Herndon Davis, noted Western artist, painted a wash drawing (opposite) of the notorious House of Mirrors in 1936. A write-up accompanied the drawing, printed in the Rocky Mountain News, which offered still another interpretation of the heads, but similar to that of Lee Casey's column, given in the text. The building served as the Buddhist Church of Denver (see sign in the window) from 1929 until 1948 when Royal Judd bought it to turn into a warehouse. John C. O'Flaherty acquired the bust of Jennie Rogers to use as a decorative piece for a garden wall at his residence in Cherry Hills. The triangular portrait was four feet high, five feet at the base, and weighed about two hundred pounds. It was badly decayed by the weather, and he laminated the sculpture with silicone in an effort to preserve it. But all was in vain. Jennie fell into pieces when she was lifted into the garden wall—almost as if the imperious madam had ruled only a queen's niche would do.

Mattie Silks of Denver

A petite madam who turned into the darling of every masculine author dealing with Denver's scandalous red-light district—that was Mattie Silks.

Since Forbes Parkhill has covered her story fully in *The Wildest of the West* and she has been the main protagonist of a paperback besides appearing in many other books, I'll give her biography only in outline.

Madam Silks made her Colorado debut by opening a parlor house in Georgetown in the 1870s. (Incidentally Mattie Silks preferred to be called a *madame*, which she thought was tonier, despite the French word's being entirely incorrect in this usage.) She arrived with a bevy of girls, having previously operated parlor houses in the wild cattle-shipping towns of Kansas. It was her boast that she had always been a "madame," never a "boarder."

By 1877 she had moved her operation to Denver where she soon began to appear in the newspapers. First the police accounts told of her being drunk and paying a fine in March, and then in August of her fighting a duel with a rival madam, Kate Fulton. A number of different versions appeared at the time, and the facts are probably lost.

Apparently Mattie was jealous because Kate was romancing with Cortez D. Thomson, a foot racer, whom Mattie considered her man. At an outing in the Denver Park, outside the city limits, the women shot at and missed each other. But in the ensuing drunken brawl of seconds to the duel, friends, spectators and hack drivers, Cort Thomson was nicked by a bullet in the neck. Kate was kicked and received a broken nose, and several other participants were battered and bruised.

"MADAME" M. SILKS

Phillip McCourt's crony said this fashion model bore a distinct resemblance to Mattie, and it does suggest the photo opposite, except the ears. Mattie may have been petite but her ears were certainly not. Even the little girl who resembles her in the family photo has the same big ears as in both those of Mattie. The old-timer insisted that his clipping was true even to the usual necklace with pendant cross and that his one of Jennie Rogers also displayed her emerald earrings, almost a trademark. The fashion model he thought looked like Jennie was reproduced on Page 8.

The newspapers considered the whole affair "a disgraceful occurrence of the fast element." The court later dismissed all charges as unproved. Whether the two women actually did shoot at each other, no one knows. Still, the questionable story lives on sturdily, insisting that they did shoot and did remain enemies until Kate's disappearance.

What survived in truth was Mattie's love for Cort Thomson whom she married in 1884. After he lost his prowess as a foot racer, he turned to being a sports manager. But his main interests were not centered on such practical money-making matters. Gambling, drinking and confidence games were more to his liking even though he was consistently unlucky at these unhealthy pursuits. Cort just relied on Mattie to bail him out.

Mattie always did. She had learned to be a very successful business woman, and she loved Cort despite his many infidelities, gambling losses and drunken cruelties to her. By 1880 Mattie was installed in her own

MATTIE SILKS

The petite madam was pretty and plump most of her life. She had naturally curly very light brown hair with golden streaks in it which darkened with age. She is remembered by old-timers as wearing a cross most of the time. One of those crosses was diamond-studded and was purchased from the estate of Lizzie Preston, not the one shown here.

parlor house at 500-502 Holladay (later 1916-22 Market) Street which she ran steadily until 1912. For twenty-two years in this house (which was really two houses connected at the rear) she maintained an enviable position in the red-light district. She was the most stable and consistent high-class madam Denver ever had.

By "stable" I do not mean that in her early days in Colorado she did not indulge in drunks and tempestuous scenes (especially the duel over Cort). I do mean that after Mattie selected the property at 1916-22 Market in 1880, the city tax rolls carried this address in her name consistently for forty-two years. She did not play "musical chairs" as often as did the other madams on The Row.

Except for her five-year move to the House of Mirrors and for the two years of 1878-79 just previous to her acquiring 1916-22 Market, when she was listed across the street at a house that was not as substantial as her final choice, her directory listing was stationary. Having

IS THIS THE FAMILY OF MATTIE SILKS?

This photo was found in the basement of 1942 Market. The little girl bears a striking resemblance to Mattie—perhaps a rumored daughter?

made her decision, Mattie stayed with it. At first she leased and then in 1884 bought the brick half of her two-dwelling house for $14,000. (She had already bought the frame side of her house in 1880, probably using in part the $4,600 Jennie Rogers had paid her that January for Mattie's small brick house, 2009 Market, which Mattie had bought only for investment purposes.)

Mattie was twenty-nine years old when she began to operate in Denver. The petite shady lady was experienced far beyond her years, having first chosen her role of "madame" as a nineteen-year-old. That was during the troubled year following the Civil War.

Mattie had been born and brought up in Indiana and claimed she opened her first house in 1866 in Springfield, Missouri. Later Olathe, Abilene, Hays City and Dodge City knew her in her chosen role. She even went into the freighting business for a time and probably made her first trip to Denver in 1869 in connection with this venture. During these years she moved often, operating her houses in the summers and spending her winters in cities like Kansas City and Chicago.

It was in Chicago that she first saw Cort Thomson. He was a professional foot racer, a Texan with reddish-blond hair and moustache. His body was compactly and gracefully built. The swaggering Texan was matched against a famous sprinter of the day, but Mattie liked Cort's looks and put her money on him. She won so heavily against the favorite that her handbag would not hold her winnings. She had to convert the skirt of her dress into a carryall by holding it up for the losers to drop in their bets.

After the race Cort and Mattie met and instantly fell in love. At the time Cort was married and had a daughter, and Mattie was involved in a common-law marriage with a man by the name of Silks. The actual identity of Silks is moot. He may have been a professional gambler, George W. Silks, who was a dealer in Georgetown, Denver and Leadville in the 1870s and early '80s, and then disappeared. He may have been Casey Silks, a railroad man, whom Mattie knew in Missouri in 1866 when she was operating her first house. According to Mattie's Negro maid, this common-law marriage lasted thirteen years, and Mattie had a child by Silks. (Perhaps George W. and Casey are the same man which would span the years from 1866 to the 1879 Leadville rush when Silks left Mattie in Denver.)

Certainly she used the name "Silks" for all legal transactions up to 1884, signing her name, Martha A. Silks. Whatever her marital status

MATTIE POSED WITH A FAVORITE RACEHORSE

For many years Mattie had a place on West Forty Fourth Ave. where Frank Nott trained her horses. The younger woman is not identified.

may have been, the rumors about her having a daughter persisted until The Row was closed. Whether this was true or was some confusion with Cort's daughter, we will never know. But the little girl shown on page 36 has Mattie's same light brown curly hair, tilted nose and big ears. If the clothes in the photograph were right for the mid-1850s instead of much later, we could be sure the child was Mattie, herself.

When Mattie changed her base of operations from the Midwest to Georgetown, Colorado, Cort turned up shortly after. He had been in San Francisco, still cutting a dash with two pistols hung on his hips, but not making out financially. No doubt he thought he had better get closer to Mattie's soft heart and open purse. He continued his professional footracing, joined a volunteer fire department and gambled with George Silks who was running a den. When Mattie moved to Denver in 1876, Silks and Thomson made a similar move to the city. With The Row rip-roaring, they all fitted in nicely.

After Mattie's marriage to Cort in Peru, Indiana, in 1884, she concentrated more and more on business. She drank only champagne, and that in moderation—no more drunken sprees. She was still capable of losing her temper over Cort's infidelities and tried to shoot Lillie Dab, one of his paramours. Cort wrested the pistol from her hand and beat Mattie cruelly. In retaliation she filed for divorce but supinely withdrew the suit. Mostly she ran her house and made money.

Occasionally she took summer trips with her girls, hauling along a big tent to set up for temporary business in such mining camps as Jimtown, or later in the Klondike. Once she took Cort and a few of her favorites on a non-working respectable spree to England. Mostly she spent her profits on Cort's troubles, harness horses, her stable of race horses, and finally on a ranch at Wray, Colorado. This property was bought mainly as a ruse to keep Cort out of Denver and hopefully out of debt. The ruse was not entirely successful although it eased Mattie's troubles somewhat. Cort died there in April, 1900, and Mattie, faithful to the end, had him buried in Denver's Fairmount Cemetery.

Mattie continued running her house through the early 1900s as she added to her fortune. She had a big jolly bouncer who was called Handsome Jack Ready. He was a flamboyantly flashy dresser, loving diamonds so much that he had a big one set in a front tooth. Formerly he had been a telegrapher, and as he made himself increasingly useful to Mattie, he moved up to being bookkeeper for her house. By 1923 he was living in Mattie's hideaway residence at 2635 Lawrence and by 1924, when Mattie was seventy-six years old, they were married.

During the passage of these years the temper of Denver changed radically. A serious movement to shut down Market Street began in 1910. Harassment of parlor houses and saloons became more severe. Mattie thought nothing would come of it, that the crusade would blow over. She believed so implicitly in her business that in January, 1911, she decided on expansion rather than curtailment.

For $14,000 she purchased the infamous House of Mirrors from the estate of Jennie Rogers who had died a year and a quarter before. Now Mattie was undisputed Queen of the Red-light District once again. So that all might know, she had her named installed in tile on the front stoop—M. Silks.

Mattie's triumph was short-lived. Three years after her expansion the state of Colorado voted for prohibition. In the following year, 1915, the Denver authorities shut down Market Street so tightly The Row was called "Pad-lock Alley." Mattie still hung on, trying to operate 1916-22 Market street as a legitimate hotel with a sly chambermaid call-girl service on the side. Due to the hotel's location that idea was a failure.

Resigned and beaten, Mattie gave up. She sold the House of Mirrors in November, 1919. Ten years later it was resold to the Denver Buddhist Church, and still another ten years later, Mattie came to her end in the Denver General Hospital. She was eighty-one years old and was buried in Fairmount Cemetery under a headstone "Martha A. Ready, January 7, 1929." It stands beside the unmarked grave of Cortez D. Thomson.

Her large estate had dwindled to a net value of only a couple of thousand dollars. So the petite madam, good business woman though she may have been, ended up petite in every respect.

MATTIE PROCLAIMED HER TRIUMPH IN TILE

It was extremely rare for the parlor houses to have any indication but numbers. Mattie broke the rule on acquiring Jennie's palace.

Laura Evans of Salida

Miss Laura was a hoyden—she specialized in pranks, wiles, peccadillos and boisterous drunks—anything for a laugh. She was as unregenerate a sporting girl as you could meet. If St. Paul was right in his *Epistle to the Romans*: "The wages of sin is death," he did not know Miss Laura would be along. When she died in Salida, April 6, 1953, she lacked only seven weeks of being ninety-one years old.

To the end, she rolled her own cigarettes, called a spade a steam shovel and told her stories of the underworld (some of them inaccurate and malicious) with unabashed heartiness and enjoyment. She swore, used bad language and was generous to a fault. Despite her mercurial disposition her girls adored her, and she had many friends in Salida unconnected with her business (which was shut down by Chaffee County authorities in 1950). At the time of her death she was something of a town institution.

Laura Evans had been a beauty in her youth. From then on she always retained that assurance which beauty and good health give the owner. It was she who condemned Mattie Silks' house as "The Old Ladies' Roost" because Mattie was loyal to her old girls and would not dismiss them after they had passed their youthful attractiveness. It was also Laura who contended that the astute business woman, Jennie Rogers, could not read nor write, which research has since contradicted. Perhaps Laura was jealous of these successful madams and chose to vent her spleen, or maybe she just wanted to be impressive and colored her stories accordingly—about them and herself.

She admitted to having a Southern background, to marrying at the age of seventeen, deserting her husband and daughter, changing her name, and turning prostitute in St. Louis. She was in her late twenties when she moved into Colorado and tried Market Street for a few years, working in different parlor houses. In the early '90s she left for Leadville and spent two or three riotous years in that wild mining camp. Many of her stories dated from the Leadville period.

Ringling Brothers' circus came to town, and Laura immediately spotted some wonderful-looking horses—three blacks and three whites. It did not take Laura long to find out that these high-spirited animals were used in a Roman chariot act. She thought it would be fun to have a chariot race up State Street and down Harrison Avenue, the main street of Leadville, instead of as a mere part of the paid performance. She persuaded Spuddy, a girl who worked in the same parlor house as Laura, that this really was a brilliant scheme.

40

The next afternoon the girls had a few drinks before going to the circus grounds. They tried to hire the chariots for $5 each. The hostlers refused. Laura, who loved horses and her own way, tipped a boy to take the elephants' water bucket to a saloon and bring it back full of beer. When she presented this delightful surprise to the hostlers, they relented. They accepted the refreshment and the money. The chariots were hitched up, and the girls were strapped in, even to fastening their feet to the floor. Off they went at a lively clip.

"Was I ever proud, with everybody looking at us! Hot dog!" Laura reminisced. "Man, if you ever want to have fun, just get tight and run a chariot race down your main street. Katie, bar the door!"

(This last was an exclamation that Laura liked to use when she was making an effort to be refined. She was capable of much tougher talk but, when she was playing raconteur, she sounded out her audience first to be sure they could take her in full stride.)

Laura turned a corner too fast, smashed into a telephone pole, tipped the chariot over and wrecked it. The police arrived and were about to put her in jail. Happily, at that moment one of Leadville's leading citizens, who was not averse to a little fun and visited the parlor houses regularly, happened along. He persuaded the police to let her go.

Two more of her escapades involved her horsemanship—or lack of it. She and Spuddy, Laura said, were looking for amusement when something got into them—probably champagne. It was the winter of 1896 when Leadville had erected a fabulous palace of ice blocks. Statues, minarets and castellated walls were carved entirely of ice, rising at the towers as high as ninety feet. It cost the town some $200,000 and was designed as a tourist attraction, with exhibits of Leadville ore specimens and local handiwork. An ice skating rink and a ballroom were parts of its enormous interior. Here music and beer kept everyone's spirits in good form.

Laura and Spuddy decided another visit to the Ice Palace wouldn't do them any harm. They hired a sleigh, drawn by a horse named Broken-Tail Charlie, and drove straight into the entrance of the Ice Palace, instead of tying the horse to the hitching post.

"Broken-Tail Charlie got scared at the music and kicked hell out of our sleigh and broke the shafts and ran away and kicked one of those four-foot ice pillars all to pieces and ruined the exhibits before he ran home to his stable," Laura finished in a burst of speed.

Her second horsemanship story dated from the same year: A strike occurred at the Maid of Erin mine, although not all the miners walked off the job. A heavy guard of union sympathizers, armed with Winchesters, was thrown around the mine. These men completely stopped traffic on or off the premises, and the owners could not drive in with the payroll. One owner asked Laura if she would smuggle the necessary money to the superintendent.

41

Laura agreed. Since no woman rode astride in those days and every horsewoman had a full-skirted sidesaddle habit, Laura took the canvas bag with impunity. It contained twenty-seven thousand dollars. She fastened the bag to the inside of her skirt just below where her leg rested on the sidesaddle horn and rode off up Carbonate Hill. When the guard stopped her and asked where she was going Laura answered honestly:

"The Maid of Erin mine. I want to see a friend that you fellows won't let come down to town."

The payroll went through easily. Its delivery broke the back of the strike, and in gratitude the principal owner asked her to dinner at his home in Denver, when she was down. Later at a sumptuous formal affair, he passed her off as a stenographer and gave her a $100 bill when she left.

Miss Laura enjoyed "crossing over," as the saying was for passing one's self off as a good woman. One time she was visiting a madam friend of hers in Central City, Della Warwick. A charity masquerade was scheduled at the Teller House to raise funds for a worthy cause. Laura dressed herself as a nun, played her role perfectly, and was never suspected. So successful was her prank that she was afraid no one would believe her story and decided to have herself photographed in the habit. This photo shows her as a very nice-looking woman whose soulful eyes were her most prominent feature.

Even late in life, when extreme age had taken its toll, her large eyes were still expressive, scintillating or saddened in concert with her talk. Her figure was bone-thin, when I met her in Salida, yet vibrant with an inner vitality. When we arrived on Front Street for our call, she was playing *panguingui,* a card game much favored in parlor houses because a girl could lay down her hand, retreat to her bedroom for a date, return a short time later, and enter the game again without a hitch.

Miss Laura was not playing with her girls—they had been banished nearly three years before. She had rented their rooms to railroad men who gathered around at night in her former parlor to play cards. Miss Laura was the only woman in the house except for a cleaning-woman who came in each morning. She found this amusing except for being pestered by the doorbell. She had been forced to tack up a sign *No More Girls.*

Her living quarters were centered in a large bedroom on the main floor opposite the parlor where the men played cards. The room was dominated by a large four-poster canopied bed covered with a frilly counterpane, feminine pillows and several very large dolls. Her dressing table had knicknacks and mementoes strewn over it, and the walls and corners were equally filled. She sat in a large leather chair, and there were a number of other comfortable chairs about the room; one, a rocker. The furniture was a mixture both in taste and periods, as was everything else in the room, from a big Teddy Bear to the statue of a horse.

42

LAURA EVANS RULED FROM HER BEDROOM

This was Laura's favorite leather chair where she sat, continuously smoking and chatting. The artist included only a few of her keepsakes.

Miss Laura had lived right where she was for fifty-two years. She had left Leadville toward the end of 1896. According to one story, her part in the Maid of Erin strike led to a blacklisting by the miners' union. Her diminished popularity made her seek a town that had a large population of men other than miners. Salida, at that time, was a perfect choice. It was a rail center for the *Denver and Rio Grande Railroad*, busy with shops, roundhouse, and switching activities. She was an immediate success.

Up to that time Laura spent money as fast as she made it, flinging it around on $150 gowns, champagne busts, and trips to Denver. It was her love for horses that finally made her think of saving enough to own a good riding horse, instead of renting regularly from a livery stable. As she got used to the idea of hanging on to her money, her ambition rose from owning horses to owning a parlor house.

43

THE HOUSE

Laura's Front Street parlor house is now a club for the Mon-Ark Shrine Lodge.

In 1900 she left "The Line" and opened her large Front Street parlor house as a full-fledged madam. As Miss Laura prospered, in 1906 she acquired the row of cribs directly opposite her house for further revenue. She became a minor power in town politics, and many a man dropped in to talk with her without regard to her "boarders." A realist to the core, she spoke her mind frankly on local issues and was never more successful than during the severe flu epidemic of 1918.

Salida was very badly hit. There were not enough nurses, and the hospital was too crowded to admit another patient.

"Tell you what I'll do," Laura suggested to the authorities and to Dr. George Curfman. "I'll shut down the house and cribs. You get the girls nurses' aid uniforms, and I'll send them around to help wherever Dr. Curfman wants. Sure, they aren't trained nurses, but they can help some. Keep it a secret."

One very pretty girl, later given the nickname of Silver Heels Jessie, was sent to nurse the minister's wife. The woman was so sick she was not expected to live. The pretty "boarder" stayed with her patient night and day until the crisis was past, both nursing and cooking. After some weeks, the woman was diagnosed as recovering. The minister was so grateful to the fine young nurse that he wanted her to stay on as housekeeper and companion to his wife.

"No," the pretty girl answered. "Now that my job is done, I'll be on my way back to Miss Laura's on Front Street."

The minister was flabbergasted. It was he who had been most fanatic in leading a crusade to shut down Front Street. That was the end of that particular crusade.

Laura's house stayed open longer than any other in Colorado, due largely to the unusual qualities of its owner. After the town council passed the final edict, Salida began to have assaults on the streets. The council came back to her and suggested that she re-open.

THE CRIBS

Laura's cribs, across the street, are now respectable small apartments, well-kept.

"No, it's too late now," Miss Laura replied. "I like my railroad-men roomers, and they're all settled in."

Miss Laura died as she had lived in full possession of her faculties, rolling and smoking her own cigarettes, looking out the window where the Angel of Shavano would be made by unmelted snow on the mountainside later in the year, and leaving all her property to her daughter.

She was buried in a pinon grove on a changeable April day, reminding the score of mourners at her funeral of the coffin's occupant. As the day blew a shift of snow down the Arkansas Valley, followed by dark rolling clouds and then clear blue Colorado sunshine, more than one person thought of Laura's swift moving moods.

All at once a burst of sunlight caught the glistening tops of the Sawatch Range as if some current or spirit had swiftly risen up and floodlighted them. It was almost as if Miss Laura were up to another prank—a prank similar to the one when she had gone into the lobby of the Vendome Hotel in Leadville with a wealthy patron. There in front of her was the elevator—a rarity, the only one in town.

What a marvelous toy! Laura insisted on taking command despite the fact that she knew nothing about its mechanism. First she stuck the elevator between floors while the hotel manager ran up the stairs, from floor to floor, shouting directions and trying to avert a crisis. But the manager was too late. Laura shot the elevator up so fast it nearly went through the roof.

Luckily the elevator jammed at the top of the well, and both Laura and the cage were finally rescued. Through the years this episode remained one of her favorite recollections, and every mourner by the graveside knew the story. It just might be that Miss Laura was choosing to ascend heavenward over the snow-topped mountains by some similar ghostly strategy—a prankster for St. Peter.

❧◖◗❧

Lillian Powers of Florence

Lillian Powers was unique among madams because she gloried in having been a crib girl, and until the day of her death, claimed she preferred a crib operation. Mostly the madams and "boarders" were contemptuous of the crib girls because parlor house inmates were considered the social hierarchy by all the tenderloin. But not Miss Lil. She told me so at *Lil's Place* in November, 1952. There she had been the madam from 1920 until 1950 when Fremont County irrevocably closed her establishment.

At the time of our call Miss Lil was living all by herself in her big rambling house close to the railroad tracks. She must have been in her late seventies because she was eighty-seven when she died in a nursing home eight years later. She certainly did not show her age. Her clear complexion with its firm flesh, and trim, though stocky, figure made me think of her as a good fifteen years younger.

Miss Lil talked to us for nearly three hours. Her manner was dignified and her English rather well chosen. In fact, when I complimented her on her vocabulary, she laughed and said:

"You know when I was young in Wisconsin, I was pressed into being the school teacher in a one-room school house. At least temporarily."

I could easily believe it. She showed in her manner the remnants of quite a little education.

Miss Lil made me promise that nothing she said would be used in print during her lifetime since her relatives in Wisconsin were unaware of what her life in Colorado had actually been. After she received our promise, she talked with unabashed openness.

Lillian had come from sturdy farm stock, probably Swedish. She had not liked the hard work and particularly the loneliness of such a life. So when she was about seventeen, she had left home and gone to a nearby town to work in the Eureka Laundry. She did not specify the town. I assumed it may have been Minneapolis because later she spoke of knowing Minnesota, Wisconsin, and South Dakota. At the Eureka she did such excellent work with her ironing and finishing that she became known as "The Laundry Queen." This recollection amused her, and obviously she was flattered that her boss and co-workers had given her such a nickname.

Shortly after her laundry job, or perhaps while she was still working at the Eureka, she joined "the profession" of her own free will. She explained that in the 1890s women could be school teachers,

46

housemaids or do menial work in a plant such as the one in which she was working; but they were forever limited to a very dull life. The kind of marriage available to a poor farm girl or plant worker offered no better. Miss Lil wanted something gay, and she laughed again as she looked back on the girl she had been.

Several years passed while she plied her trade in the general area of her childhood—Wisconsin, Minnesota and the Dakotas, working westward all the time. In South Dakota she met mining men, who had an entirely different viewpoint from the farmers and townsmen she had known. They kept telling her about Colorado, and particularly Cripple Creek. They said it was really the town of opportunity, lots of free-spending miners and over-night millionaires; gold was popping out of the mountains all around.

Miss Lil, who was always the frugal type, had saved some money and decided to come West. She told me that she stopped only a short time in Denver and was not impressed. The dance hall girls at the Alcatraz Theatre (on the northeast corner of 20th and Market Streets) were making only 50c an evening and they had to be on their feet all night. The crib girls were cutting prices and that made it hard for her. So Lillian kept on toward her goal. She took the narrow-gauge *Denver and Rio Grande* to Colorado Springs and there changed to the *Short Line* which brought her into Victor, the rich sister mining camp of Cripple Creek.

Lillian operated in Victor for several months (or years — exact dates were always hazy). Then she transferred to Cripple Creek where she rented a corner crib in a row owned by a madam known as Leo-the-Lion. Lillian explained that at the time Leo-the-Lion was going down hill, drinking a lot and flying into violent rages. The madam had formerly run a sporting house on Cripple Creek's infamous Myers Avenue, made some money and invested it in real estate, particularly the row of cribs. By the time Miss Lil knew her, Leo had lost out on the carriage trade, given up the house and was working as a crib girl in one of her own cribs.

"I made good right away," Miss Lil said and went on to explain that it was her habit to keep her crib very attractive. She always had a nice spread and clean linen on the bed, clean towels hung on the washstand, and frilly curtains at the window. Her idea was to create a pleasant atmosphere, and she even let the regular men sit down, drink beer (at a profit), and talk to her of their troubles while she listened sympathetically. Nearly always she made higher tips and took in more money this way than if she tried to rush every customer in and out. Also, by this method, she built a clientele that came back night after night.

Business went along briskly, and Lil was quite happy. But as the months passed, Leo grew increasingly jealous of the young woman's trade and said Lillian shouldn't hog all the good beer-drinking busi-

LILLIAN POWERS WAS BLONDE AND JOLLY

A formal portrait, probably done when Lil was still a crib girl and designed for sale to customers, showed her beautiful hair and shoulders. Many crib girls and parlor house girls posed for formal photographs which were later used as part of their business. These pictures often showed the girls full-length and dressed in an elaborate stylish outfit of the day. As sentimental mementoes, they were undistinguishable from any ordinary photograph. The pictures were never suggestive and, if discovered later in the man's effects, in no way implicated the purchaser as having been involved in a clandestine or adulterous act.

ness. One of the men who had been a big spender at Leo-the-Lion's house, and was still patronizing the madam personally, began to come to Lillian. The man agreed that for discretion's sake he would use Lillian's back door, and this plan worked for a long time. But then Leo-the-Lion found out that her favorite customer had been sneaking into Lillian's crib. In a fit of temper, she started drinking that morning and kept at it all day. By evening she was in a towering rage and headed down the street for the corner crib.

"You double-crossing bitch," she screamed, pounding on Lillian's door, "you get out, and I mean "get out." You get out of this crib and out of town. Or I'll kill you!"

Lillian peeked out the window and saw that the drunken Leo with her bushy leonine hair was flourishing a pistol. The crib girl was genuinely frightened. She fled out the back door and up to the telephone office, hoping to get there before it closed. She just made it in time.

"Please get me Miss Laura Evans in Salida," she told the operator.

It took quite awhile for the long distance call to be put through. But finally she had Salida's most prominent madam on the wire. Lillian explained that she was leaving Cripple Creek immediately and asked Miss Laura if she could come to Salida and rent one of her cribs.

"Sure. Come on," Miss Laura replied in her throaty voice.

Lillian hired a young boy to help her pack and get her on the train. It would have been shorter to go by way of the *Florence and Cripple Creek Railroad*. But Lillian wanted to be gone by dawn, and the earliest train went to Colorado Springs. So Lillian and the boy worked all night, assembling everything in a large trunk, a satchel and a hat box. Most of the extra furnishings in the crib were hers, and Lillian thought they would never get the lid closed on all her belongings. The boy got her luggage loaded onto a hack, while she, herself, carried a large purse with considerable cash folded in its various pockets. As the snow on the heights of Pikes Peak began to turn pink, and the Sangre de Cristos to the southwest were flaming rose, Lil pulled out of Cripple Creek, never to return.

Incidentally, Madam Leo and Myers Avenue were written up by Julian Street in 1914 in the November 21 issue of *Colliers*. By that time Leo-the-Lion had moved into Lillian's corner crib and hung a gold-lettered glass sign on a brass chain in the window, reading *Madam Leo*. As the author strolled by, she stepped out the door and surveyed him. Julian Street reported that Leo was dressed in a white linen skirt and a middy-blouse—attire grotesquely juvenile for a woman of her years. He added that her hair was rather thin, light brown, and stringy; that she resembled a highly respectable, if homely, German cook, and that she had a silly, noisy laugh.

He described Myers Avenue as being lined with flimsy buildings, half tumbled-down and abandoned except for one block of crowded-together one-story buildings. Instead of a number, each bore a name, "Clara," "Louise," "Lina," and so on down the block. The crib women, including one Negress, tried to lure him in, he added, along with other unflattering details. When the townspeople of Cripple Creek read the author's portrayal, they were so incensed that they met in solemn session and changed the name of Myers Avenue to Julian Street.

But to return to Lillian Powers whose flight from Myers Avenue preceded this event by some years, her journey to Salida by way of Colorado Springs was long and tiring. In addition, she had spent the whole night packing. She arrived in Salida that evening worn out and dirty. When Lillian knocked at the door of Laura Evans' parlor house on Front Street (which she had spotted because of the thumping piano and the whooping noise), a slim girl answered, surveyed her, and snottily called out to Miss Laura that there was a crib girl to see her.

"What's she look like?" Lillian could hear Miss Laura ask above the roar.

"Not much," the girl replied. "Dirty and old."

Lillian was furious but said nothing. The girl handed her a key and pointed out the crib across Front Street from the parlor house. Lillian took the key and went to the nearest saloon where she asked if anyone wanted work. An old man stepped forward. She hired him to get coal and build a fire in the stove so that she could have hot water. With the help of the old man she thoroughly scrubbed and mopped the crib (which had been left in horrible condition). After paying him, Lillian had a sponge and sitz bath, washing off all the grime and cinders of her long trip. Then she had a long restful sleep.

Early the next afternoon she put on her best white dress and airily sailed across the street to pay her rent in advance and show off what she really looked like. The slim girl (whose name turned out to be Mickey) again answered the door but she didn't recognize Lillian and called for Miss Laura. The madam arrived wearing an old-fashioned apron, her hair in long braids topped by a boudoir cap. Lillian was completely startled at her appearance.

"Are you really Miss Laura?" Lillian asked.

"Yeah, what's left of me," Miss Laura replied in her downright manner and invited Lillian in. Lillian told Miss Laura she was the new crib girl and had come to pay the rent in advance, adding that she wanted it to run from the time of her long distance call.

"Katie, bar the door," Miss Laura exclaimed in one of her favorite expressions. "Mickey didn't recognize you!"

So began a long and profitable association between the two women.

One night a customer gave Lillian a $20 gold piece. Lillian did not want to open her trunk and make change from her own store as the man might see how much she had and steal it. So she excused herself, explaining that she was nearly broke, and would go over to Miss Laura's for change. Again she was dressed in her white frilly dress and, when Miss Laura and the girls saw her nice appearance and the type

LIL'S GIRL

Pictured here are Lil and one of her boarders (who also worked for Laura in Salida). This photo was taken in the '20s when Lil was at her stoutest. As long as Lil lived, she continued to hear from past girls who gave her real devotion and fidelity. This particular girl later married and kept her sporting life a secret.

of clientele she was building up, they were really impressed. Miss Laura asked her to move across the street and become one of her parlor house girls.

But Lillian refused. She really did not like "to drink and whoop it up" and preferred her crib work, where she could make more money. When Miss Laura saw how true this was for Lillian, she turned the management of the cribs over to Lillian on a percentage basis that proved to be a real money-making arrangement for both of them.

51

During Lillian's short stay in Denver she had come to know two "big names." They had taken her out in Denver, and when they went on a mining trip to Leadville, they stopped off in Salida to see her. They asked her to go out drinking and dancing with them. But she refused on the ground that she would be losing business. They asked her if the evening was worth $20 just for companionship? She estimated that her regular business would not produce as handsome a profit as that and went out with them.

As time passed, Lillian built up a small fortune and decided to move to Florence and open her own house close to the railroad tracks. Lillian and Laura remained good friends, and the madams visited back and forth in each other's houses for many years. But Lillian's theory of running a house differed considerably from many other madams.

Lil's Place on the southern outskirts of Florence did not have many girls but concentrated on a big attractive beer garden with a high wall for privacy. She spent some $30,000 in fixing up her layout just the way she wanted it. The garden had a floor for dancing, and a small musicians' stand. On Saturday nights in summer it was probably the prettiest and gayest spot in town. When the weather was cold, Lillian also had a ballroom inside with a player piano. It was toward the back of the house on the left of a long hall which had a sitting room at the front on the right, then Lil's bedroom, followed by the dining room and kitchen. The girls' bedrooms were on the second floor and were reached by stairs on the left at the front of the long hall. The rooms I saw were clean and comfortable but none of the furnishings were memorable.

Immediately after Miss Lil opened for business she acquired a following for herself and her two or three boarders. Many of the railroad men who had patronized her in Salida found it convenient to stop off in Florence. Both they and the local men who wanted to frolic were enthusiastic about her beer garden. The townspeople varied in their attitude, and from time to time in the course of her thirty years' operation *Lil's Place* had to be shut down for a while. But the reform wave would pass, and soon again the sound of merriment and laughter floated over the wall.

Her trash hauler recalls that during the 1920s Lil grew enormously stout but that she always retained her magnetic personality. Later she reduced and maintained the same weight thereafter. About twice a year she phoned him to take away a full load of stuff, cleared from the garden and coach house.

For years she had a couple living in the coach house, the wife acting as cook and the man as general handyman. In the 1930s Lil collected a dollar a bottle for beer that cost her a dime. But if she made an exorbitant profit, she passed it on to others easily. She never quibbled with the trash hauler about his price and paid him promptly. She was also generous with her old girls. When they had passed their

52

prime and were down on their luck, they often wrote Lil or sought her out because she was an easy touch.

"After all," Lil remarked, "this is a business where you've got to make it in a few years."

The final shutdown did not come until 1950, when Fremont County's district attorney, John Stump Witcher, made the closing order stick. Lil had to send her boarders on their way and could serve no liquor. She, however, stayed on, living alone rather spookily in her mansion, doing her own cooking and going uptown very seldom. The coach house was empty of horses, cars or servants, and the beer garden was overgrown with weeds. But through the years she had kept up the house, and I asked her why she didn't rent the rooms.

"No one wants to live so close to the railroad tracks. I don't mind the trains. I kind of like them—reminds me of so many old friends. But the ordinary renter doesn't feel that way."

After our visit, Lil had better luck. She was able to find some renters, and still she lingered on, living comfortably in that same *Lil's Place* that for thirty years had been a thorn in the flesh of Florence churchgoers. Finally ill health forced Miss Lil into a nursing home, and her big parlor house was turned into apartments. It stands there still, basking in the Arkansas Valley sun, with a delightful view of the Wet Mountains over the garden wall.

Lillian Powers died in October, 1960, taking many secrets to her grave, not the least of which was how the money was made that her relatives inherited. She died with everything in order—as neat and orderly as each of her successive cribs—and, knowing her, I'm sure there were clean sheets on the bed.

LIL'S PLACE LOOKED LIKE THIS IN 1960

The railroad tracks and dilapidated crossing sign cannot obscure the charm of the enclosed garden, the flowers and the view of the mountains.

Pearl de Vere of Cripple Creek

A broken butterfly—that was Pearl de Vere—and her name and beauty were long forgotten.

When Mabel Barbee Lee's book, *Cripple Creek Days*, appeared in 1958, Mrs. Lee included a most moving chapter about Pearl de Vere, entitled *Good-bye, Little Girl, Good-bye*. The pretty madam was pictured as seen through the eyes of an eleven-year-old child who was enchanted with Pearl de Vere's looks. Unfortunately Mrs. Lee's book, supposedly based on the author's own childhood memories of the richest gold camp in the United States, does not hesitate to resort to many passages of fiction.

One instance is the date of death of the chic dainty madam. Mrs. Lee sets the poignant scene as having occurred on Christmas Eve during a lavish party and believes the unhappy lady committed suicide. Actually Pearl died on a Saturday afternoon around three o'clock, the result of having misgauged the amount of morphine to take to induce sleep. The date was June 5, 1897.

Two Cripple Creek and three Denver newspapers ran obituaries that I have been able to find—there may have been more. The *Denver Times* merely said that she was a "leader of the Cripple Creek Demi Monde" and that she died of an overdose of morphine. The others gave many details. One, which Mrs. Lee quotes, was delightfully melodramatic and suggested her death was intentional. The other three were very prosaic and flatly stated that it was an accident, confirmed by the coroner's findings.

Pearl de Vere had gone to Cripple Creek from Denver when the first slowdown of what was to be the Silver Panic of 1893 was beginning to affect business in the city. She was thirty-one years old.

According to the *Rocky Mountain News*, Miss Pearl was "well-known in Denver as Mrs. Martin, and at one time she was quite wealthy." In Cripple Creek she took a small frame house on Myers Avenue and became "one of the denizens of the tenderloin." Business was booming in the gold camp to the delight of Pearl, and she was patronized with princely popularity.

It is not clear whether this first operation was a very small parlor house or a high class crib. But it provided Pearl with the money to hire She Devil from Welty's Livery Stable. She Devil was known to spook at the slightest rustle of a paper and to shy with nimble quick-

54

PEARL'S "OLD HOMESTEAD" IS NOW A MUSEUM

The Fred Mentzers have restored Pearl de Vere's parlor house with turn-of-the-century furniture and a notable collection of objects to re-create its former scarlet atmosphere. In the lower photo notice the characteristic "fainting" couch. The period costumes on posed mannequins give the tourist a good idea of how Pearl and her girls looked.

THE BED

One of Pearl's girls prepares to undress for her customer.

ness. This did not bother Pearl. Riding sidesaddle in a trim, full habit with a small derby hat cocked over her heavily lashed eyes, she seemed to enjoy every moment of her precarious ride.

Her business soon provided Pearl with enough money to buy a team of prancing blacks and a single-seated phaeton. The harness had shiny clanking chains to call attention to spinning red wheels that gleamed in the sunlight as well as to the auburn-haired driver. Every day the little lady appeared in a different rich costume. She was a lovely sight—a sight to make the miners on the sidewalks stare with longing.

One miner, C. B. Flynn, stared the hardest and put his stare into action. In 1895 he married Pearl. Not long after they were married, a raging fire destroyed a large portion of Cripple Creek, wiping out the entire business section as well as Pearl's house.

According to one old-timer, C. B. Flynn was more of a millman than a miner and had invested in a small mill. It burned in the great fire and ruined him financially. Flynn decided to go back to his former job of smelting iron and steel. He accepted a job at Monterrey, Mexico.

Pearl refused to go with him. Why, no one knows. Probably it was agreeable with him or perhaps they quarreled briefly. In any case, she stayed in Cripple Creek while the town hustled and hurried to rebuild. The thriving camp, now a city, not only erected business blocks and banks and all the appurtenances of a full-blown economy, but it also rebuilt Myers Avenue, the red-light district.

The most splendid addition to The Row of 1896 was a two-story brick parlor house, humorously named The Old Homestead. Pearl became the "proprietress," as one obituary put it. She imported wallpaper from Paris and chose the most opulent furnishings to set against this unique background. Everything was of top quality—in-

56

THE TRUNK

*The girls never were
separated from their
trunks, dear safes.*

cluding two bathrooms when most people were still using privies.
Four girls joined Pearl in making her parlor house the most whispered-
about place in town.

Parties at The Old Homestead were lavish—even exotic. They
were made so by gifts of tropical flowers sent by Flynn (although how
the orchids, jasmine and acacia could survive the long journey from
Mexico has never been explained). Pearl's customers included a number of rich Denver men who made frequent business trips to Cripple
Creek. They brought her handsome gifts and liked to come to The
Old Homestead to whoop it up. Not that they were unusual; most of
Cripple Creek liked to whoop it up there, too—and why not? Millionaires were being coined by the dozen. With all the excitement, it was
a time to celebrate.

One Friday night Pearl had too much to drink. Mrs. Lee implies
that that evening a very special party was in progress. "Cases of
French champagne, caviar from Russia and crates of wild turkey
from Alabama" had been sent her by one of the new millionaires of
Poverty Gulch. Two orchestras had arrived from Denver and were
filling the night with revelry. Pearl was exquisite in "an eight-hundred-
dollar ball gown of shell pink chiffon encrusted with sequins and seed
pearls, sent to her direct from Paris."

Then the madam excused herself, went upstairs all alone, took
morphine and died. Her frail body, still draped in its chiffon ball
gown, was found on her bed by the wealthy patron of the affair. He
hastily left for Denver. Later an anomymous communication, post-
marked Denver, arrived at the undertaker's, *Fairley Bros. and Lamp-
man.* It contained a thousand dollars in crisp new bills to pay all
burial costs. The funeral that followed, as described by Mrs. Lee, is
sheer poetry and will bring tears to the reader's eyes. I recommend
her account with enthusiasm.

But, alas, I'm a historian.

Let me quote a section of the obituary of June 10, 1897 from the files of the present *Cripple Creek Gold Rush*:

"The inmates of the house had been jollifying the night previous, and it was morning before they retired. Pearl complained that her nerves were all unstrung and insisted that one of the girls should come and sleep in her room. It was eleven o'clock when the girl awoke and found Pearl lying on her face breathing heavily. She soon saw something was wrong and called for help. Dr. Hereford was summoned and did everything in his power, but the drug had been at work too long, and at three o'clock she died . . .

"A deputy sheriff took possession of The Old Homestead, one of the most elegant houses of ill repute in the city. He had all the girls move out, and placed a guard over the valuables . . ."

With only minor variations the other obituaries confirm this report. They added that she was from Evansville, Indiana, where her mother and sister were still residing. Both they and C. B. Flynn had been notified.

Mrs. Lee says the sister arrived at the mortuary and proved to be a thin sharp-nosed woman. The sister was shocked and horrified to find Pearl was a harlot with dyed red hair. Furious at the undertaker for having let her make the long trip from Indiana on such a vain mission, the sister flounced out and refused all responsibility.

The Cripple Creek old-timer, who remembers Flynn, says he thinks Pearl's husband sent the money to bury her, but probably not more than a $100. Only thirty-six years old, she was laid to rest in the Mt. Pisgah graveyard, and soon completely forgotten.

After *Cripple Creek Days* appeared, numberless tourists became interested in her story and wanted to find her headstone. A Miss Alice Peterson of Illinois was finally successful. It was almost hidden by weeds in a corner of the graveyard and was merely a simple wooden slab. The carving of the name had nearly eroded away. Miss Peterson gave the slab to the Cripple Creek Museum, and Richard Johnson of Cripple Creek started a campaign to replace the wooden marker with something more permanent.

The Wilhelm Monument Company donated a heart-shaped stone of white marble which says only "Pearl de Vere. Died. June 5, 1897." Johnson gathered enough granite stones from all the famous mines of the district and ringed the grave in an artistic oblong.

Wild rose bushes grow on top of the grave. Their deep pink color and sweet fragrance are well suited to the memory of Pearl. For years to come, the bushes will drop their petals annually, commemorating the sad tale of the wild rose who lies beneath.

Cock-Eyed Liz of Buena Vista

In the 1880s Buena Vista was a rowdy town. During this decade three railroads forged their way to or across its outskirts. The incoming railroad men added their brawling to the roistering already in full swing by freighters and miners. Buena Vista had no mines of its own, but it was the nearest shipping point for many camps nestled in the Collegiate Range. Miners drove in with ore and out with supplies every day. For a couple of years its road to the west over Cottonwood Pass offered the best route for reaching the amazing new bonanza town of Aspen. Buena Vista was a hub of activity.

It did not take long for the word to get around. One day in 1886 a rather rawboned but handsome young woman, dressed in the height of fashion, stepped off a *Denver and Rio Grande* train. She had traveled up the Arkansas Valley from Pueblo and spoke of the scenic Royal Gorge as she alighted. In the baggage car she had three trunks full of swishing taffetas and satiny silks, and in her own hands she clutched a carpet bag and a hat box. Not a single man at the depot had the least doubt of what she was—her painted face told them. No respectable woman would be seen with the least touch of makeup.

She hired a hack to the hotel, signed the register "Lizzie Spurgen," and saw to the disposal of her luggage. Then Lizzie asked to be shown lots that might be for sale. She found what she wanted on the north side of main street, just west of the former courthouse.

Here she built a one-story brick house which she called a "Palace of Joy." The parlor was on the right of the entrance, and accommodations for four girls besides herself were to the west and rear. She employed a white woman cook and a woman piano player, both of whom stayed with her for years.

At the time, Lizzie Spurgen was twenty-nine years old. She was about five-feet-seven-inches tall with dark brown hair, blue eyes and a very white velvety skin. Many of my informants stressed the fine texture of her skin, and everyone spoke of what a "fancy dresser" she was.

She said nothing about her wealth or her past except that she was "from the East" and had heard that Colorado would be good for her health. Her death certificate said she was born in Kansas; her mother, in England; her father in Virginia, but no names were given. Elizabeth Spurgen may easily have been her real name since this hardly seems the type of name a "frail sister" would assume deliberately. She was also speaking the truth about her health. All her life she was susceptible to bronchitis and during the last ten years, to severe attacks of asthma.

59

SHADY LADY

Cock-Eyed Liz was always known as a very fancy dresser when she was running her rowdy Palace of Joy in Buena Vista. Her left eye never recovered from the blow of a brawler.

Her house immediately became the center of Buena Vista night life. No one remembers how she recruited her girls but the "boarders" materialized as soon as her house was finished. There was another madam in town, Belle Brown, who resented the success of her new rival and attempted to foment trouble. One Saturday night she is said to have gotten the worst brawlers in town roaring drunk by giving them free drinks and then sent the men over to Lizzie Spurgen's to stir up a ruckus.

In the ensuing row Lizzie Spurgen was hit in one eye and blinded. She never regained the sight nor the muscular control in that eye, and was soon given the name of "Cock-Eyed Liz." Her name and her fame spread up and down the Arkansas Valley merely as "Cock-Eyed Liz and her Palace of Joy."

The girls' charge at Cock-Eyed Liz's house was $3, but it is unknown how the fee was split or if the girls paid board. (There was a wide variation in these financial arrangements from house to house and town to town.) A number of Buena Vista men remember that, as boys, the girls at Cock-Eyed Liz's would tip them a dime to take notes to the men in saloons uptown. They also recall that Liz used to hire a two-seated buggy for $5 to take her girls out for an airing in the afternoon. A "boarder" who made a deep impression was Pancake Fan, a soft-as-a-pancake girl, who left, went straight, and worked for the Salvation Army in Salt Lake.

Cock-Eyed Liz, whatever else she was, had a sense of humor. She used to say:

"A parlor house is where the girls go to look for a husband and the husbands go to look for a girl."

Liz showed her sense of humor in another way. She had a pet magpie that was kept in a cage on the front lawn. She trained the bird to greet each passer-by with:

"Come in, Boys. Come in."

One day the magpie escaped from its cage and was exploring the alley. A boy threw a rock at it, breaking the bird's leg. Liz was heartbroken and rushed her magpie to a veterinarian. The leg had to be amputated, but the bird lived to hop about on one leg and call:

"Come in, Boys. Come in."

RESPECTABLE

After Cock-Eyed Liz was married, fancy clothes had no more appeal. She dressed simply and did not primp. Callers were welcomed, as shown here with Liz, standing in front of her former Palace of Joy. The young ladies were from good families. All was forgotten.

THE PALACE

The former parlor house gives no indication today of its once lurid doings.

One man who frequented Cock-Eyed Liz's place more than any other was the town's only plumber, an Alsatian. His name was Alphonse Enderlin, whose name in Buena Vista is always pronounced Anderline. His nickname was "Foozy." "Foozy" Anderline was probably as close as the crude population of Buena Vista in the '90s could get to the French sound of Alphonse Enderlin.

Foozy liked to garden and particularly to grow fruits from which he could make wine. He did not think much of the beer, whiskey and champagne that Liz sold, preferring his own fermentations. Good-humoredly she would let him turn her kitchen into a winery even when some of the brew got too strong in the crocks and exploded.

One October Sunday morning when Colorado's Indian summer was at its most sparkling, Foozy drove up in a buggy. This was rather surprising because he generally came in his buckboard, with building and plumber's tools rattling around in back. Foozy wanted Liz to ride over to Fairplay and spend the night; said she needed a change, and Sunday-night business was always slow anyway.

Liz accepted with a smile. The year was 1897, and in a little under four months she would be forty-one years old. She was growing rather tired of whooping it up and managing the always difficult "boarders." A change was just what she needed.

It was an all-day drive to Fairplay in those days, and it was the nicest day Cock-Eyed Liz could remember. The tops of the Mosquito Range had flecks of glistening snow. South Park was soft with yellows and russets, and the Tarryalls were blue in the distance. It was a day of peace and pleasure. To cap it all, Foozy suggested they get married in the morning.

The wedding took place on Monday, October 4, in Fairplay. Cock-Eyed Liz gave her age as "over twenty one" and Foozy gave his as thirty-five. Liz was probably embarassed to admit that she was five-and-a-half years older than Foozy.

APARTMENTS

This is the wing that Foozy added to make apartments. All the building is used now.

Then they lived happily ever after.

That's a real switch for you. Imagine the leading madam of the town becoming a respectable citizen, openly living as a faithful wife in her former palace of joy! But that's what Foozy and Cock-Eyed Liz did. They let the girls go, and Foozy built a clapboard wing onto the east side of Liz's brick house. It had two apartments which they leased for steady income. They lived on the south side and occasionally they rented two of the "boarders'" former quarters to tourists. (Today the building is the Edwards Apartments.)

Foozy continued to make his wine in Liz's kitchen. He always had a tub of something that was in season brewing—dandelions, raspberries, chokecherries, gooseberries or Concord grapes. Some he picked and some he bought. The house was always full of odors, but the hospitality was genuine. Every caller was offered a glass of wine.

Along about 1910 Foozy was playing poker with some men friends in the back room of the pool hall. A man drifted in to "kibitz" and chat. He said he used to be a drummer in these parts. (Drummer was the usual term for salesman then.) He had known quite a few people around town but the place seemed changed. He idly added a few more observations.

No man at the table paid much attention to his chatter. They were intent on their game, and Foozy was dealing.

"By the way," the drummer asked, "whatever happened to Cock-Eyed Liz who used to own a sporting house here?"

You could have heard a pin drop. Every man drew in his breath and straightened in his chair—except Foozy who calmly went on dealing. Then he said flatly:

"I married her."

The drummer beat a hasty retreat. The men picked up their hands, and the card game went on as if nothing had happened.

And nothing much did happen. Cock-Eyed Liz continued her "Plain Jane" life. She, who had worn such lavish dresses, never appeared in anything except a house dress. Her hair, which had been curled and frizzed, was now snatched up on the top of her head in an ordinary knot. Yet Foozy adored her, and in her quiet way she had a number of very good friends.

When the friends came to call, she always had cookies in a jar for their children. It was an extraordinary accomplishment to have reversed her role without moving away, changing her background, or hiding her past.

This placid marriage lasted thirty-one years, Foozy consistently ignoring anything so foolish as Prohibition. Then in 1929 Liz's heart, which had been weakened by asthma attacks, gave out completely. She died in August, at the age of seventy-two, leaving Foozy heartbroken—so badly heart-broken that he had her photographed as she lay in her coffin. Gruesome as this photo might be, I should still like to see it. Unfortunately none of the former owners can now find a copy.

Five years later Foozy followed his darling to the Mt. Olivet cemetery in Buena Vista. There they lie in utter peace and respectability—a unique ending for the rowdy, racy madam named Cock-Eyed Liz.

MT. PRINCETON MAKES A PRETTY BACKGROUND

A quiet ending to the tumultuous days that created the shady ladies with their purple pasts is symbolized by this attractive monument.